# Technology for Transforming Education

## About the Editor

**Dr. Deepa Awasthi** is Doctorate in Education and Post-Graduate in Education, Sociology and Economics. She has qualified UGC-JRF in Education and Sociology as well and has equal command on both the subjects. At present she is pursuing her second Doctorate in Sociology. She has participated and presented her research papers in more than 50 national and international seminars and conferences. She also has seven edited books to her credit on various educational and sociological issues. Her publication work also involves 15 chapters in edited books, 4 research papers in form of conference and seminar proceedings and 17 research papers and articles in various journals of national and international repute. Her keen interest areas include various issues related to field of Education and Sociology.

# TECHNOLOGY FOR TRANSFORMING EDUCATION

## Emerging Trends and Issues

*Edited by*
Deepa Awasthi

**CONCEPT PUBLISHING COMPANY PVT. LTD.**
**NEW DELHI-110059**

**ISBN-13: 978-93-5125-253-5**

First Published 2017

*Published and Printed by*

Since 1974

**Concept Publishing Company Pvt. Ltd.**
**Regd. Office:**
A/15-16, Commercial Block, Mohan Garden,
New Delhi-110059 (INDIA)
*T* : 25351460, 25351794, *F* : 091-11-25357109
*Email* : publishing@conceptpub.com
*Website*: www.conceptpub.com

**Cataloging in Publication Data**--Courtesy: D.K. Agencies (P) Ltd. <docinfo@dkagencies.com>

**Technology for transforming education** : emerging trends and issues / edited by Deepa Awasthi.
pages cm
Contributed articles.
Includes bibliographical references index.
ISBN 9789351252535

1. Educational technology—India. 2. Internet in education—India. I. Awasthi, Deepa (Writer on education and sociology), editor.

LB1028.3.T43 2017 DDC 371.330954 23

# Preface

This book titled "Technology Transforming Education—Emerging Trends and Issues" is a collection of 14 chapters on the various issues related to use of technology in classroom and how this increased use of technology is affecting each and every aspects of Education. In this twenty-first century where each and every walk of life is governed by technology and new scientific inventions, It is hard to believe that field of education will go on untouched. We have entered into era of 'Power Point Presentation' from the era of 'Chalk and Slate'. Technology not only decides what to learn, but also governs how to learn. On one side use of advance technology has improved the classroom teaching; on the other side it has broken the boundaries of classroom. Students are no more bound to sit in a boring classroom and listen or write, that is being taught by teachers. He can sit anywhere in park or home and access to unlimited information available online. Technology has transformed the field of education to such limits that a student who is not present in classroom can easily learn what is being currently taught in classroom *via* video conferencing. Use of various tools and instruments have not only changed the role of teachers, but also changed the relationship between teachers and students.

Increased use of technology in education is considered differently by various academicians, experts and educationists. Some of them consider it as a method which made the task of teachers and students easy, effective, efficient and fulfilled while some of them take it as a challenging for students, teachers, school management as well as parents also. Just like the two faces of coin this technology is not only advantageous, but it has certain disadvantages associated with. The ability of technology to activate multisensory organs of human body eye, ear, brain etc. to promote multisensory instructional flow has made more popular among teachers and students as compared to other pedagogies. In few years use of technology has emerged as a single key to all the locks in field of education. It changes the direction of teaching-learning process towards learner centred from curriculum centred or teacher centred.

With the use of technology, even the children with various types of disabilities can be made learn with ease. Introduction of technology in classroom has given birth to the concept of inclusive education where children with special need can learn together with normal children and it was all possible due to learner centred approach involved in use of technology. In this continuously changing scenario the role of teachers is also changing. It is mandatory for every educator that they must remain updated with latest trends in technology around them. Appropriate and result oriented teachers' training can also play a decisive role in this regard. In India we expect every thing from teachers, but hardly ready to invest in this regard.

Although, it is well accepted that technology improves learning, but there exist a wide gap in extent of use of technology in favour of students at different stages in different countries. It is hard to expect the schools in India struggling to manage basic minimum facilities like clean and hygienic toilets, clean drinking water, appropriate and comfortable seating arrangement, availability of trained teachers and other necessary infrastructure to procure, acquire and manage world class technology for teaching their students. But it is unjust on the part of student that due to mere reason of paucity of funds thousands and millions of students remain untouched and unblessed with the advantage of use of technology in teaching-learning process. In India the use of technology in field of education is in initial stage, a long distance is to be still covered. For making sure that our schools and educational institutes march in right direction, Government must intervene and come up with a policy directing them to make a long-term plan of acquiring and using minimum standard of technology in teaching.

Apart from normal students, technology-based pedagogy is exceptionally helpful in teaching children with special needs, for example a hearing impaired can easily be taught with normal students simply by using microphone and amplifying speaker in classroom. Various other assistive technologies are also helpful to deal with the students with special need. Use of technology in classroom paces the process of learning by evoking different sensory organs. It does not mean the over dependency on technology.

This book has been prepared with the intention to detail the readers about how use of latest technology is continuously transforming each and every aspect of education. Every possible effort has been made that the content, facts and figures mentioned in book are authentic and updated.

**Dr. Deepa Awasthi**

# Acknowledgements

It is my immense pleasure to acknowledge all the learned authors who have contributed their valuable articles and research papers written by them with utmost pain, efforts and investment of time. Without their sincere and devoted thinking towards the issue of "Technology Transforming Education—Emerging Trends and Issues" it would have been almost impossible to come up with desired result. I am also obliged to the distinguished panel of reviewers who invested their precious time and hard work in evaluating the contributions from various authors and further guiding them to make their writings focused, clear and appropriate for this book. I am also thankful to all my friends, teachers and family members who encouraged me from time-to-time to remain adhered to the mission of publishing this edited book on one of the most concerned and utmost important issue about how new technologies being introduced are continuously changing the field of education.

Last but not the least, I thank to God and all who helped me directly or indirectly at every step and provided me emotional support to compile this edited book.

**Dr. Deepa Awasthi**

# Contents

# List of Contributors

**Dr. Amit Kashyap** is Doctorate in Law with 10 years teaching experience. At present he is working as Research Associate at Himachal Pradesh University, Shimla (H.P.). He is Post-graduate Diploma in Journalism and Computers, Certificate courses in Human Rights and Computers. He is First UGC-JRF/SRF in General/Male category in Department of Laws, Himachal Pradesh University, Shimla (H.P.). His keen interest involves Socio-political development of India and Issues related to women and child. He has attended and presented papers in various national and international seminars and conferences. He has published more than 40 articles and research papers in various journals. Email: amit_jura@yahoo.co.in

**Dr. Amitaraj Gargey** is Doctorate in English with 18 years teaching experience. At present she is working as Principal at Daleep Walase Arts, Science and Commerce College, Pune, Maharashtra. She is M. Phil. in Education, Diploma in German, and Certificate Course in Computers. Her keen interest involves socio-political development of India and issues related to women and child. She has attended and presented papers in various national and international seminars and conferences. She has published more than 18 articles and research papers in various journals. Email: arsh_1273@yahoo.com

**Mrs. Archana Jha** is a voracious reader and passionate writer. She had completed her Masters degree in Physics from Lalit Narayan Mithila University, Dharbhanga, Bihar and Master's in Education from Kolhan University. Currently, she is working at Institute for Education, Bijay, Seraikela (Jharkhand). Her hobbies are listening music, reading and writing. Email: archnasrishti15@gmail.com

**Dr. Deepa Awasthi** is Doctorate in Education and Post-Graduate in Education, Sociology and Economics. She has qualified UGC-JRF in

Education and Sociology as well and has equal command on both the subjects. At present she is pursuing her second doctorate in Sociology. She has participated and presented her research papers in more than 50 national and international seminars and conferences. She has seven edited books to her credit on various educational and sociological issues. Her publication work also involves 16 chapters in edited books, 4 research papers in form of conference and seminar proceedings and 17 research papers and articles in various journals of national and international repute. Her keen interest areas include the sociological issues related to women and various issues related to field of Education and Sociology. Email: dawasthi.india@gmail.com

**Dr. Meenakshi Dwivedi** is a UGC Post-doctorate Research Scholar in Department of Education, University of Lucknow, working on the Project for the Education of students suffering from Autistic Syndrome Disorder. She has completed her doctoral thesis on Pains and Gains of Visually Impaired Students Studying in Mainstream Higher Education. She is post-graduate in Education, Mathematics and Physics. She has also worked as Assistant Professor (B.Ed.) for approx seven years. She has participated and presented the papers in 14 National/International seminars and conferences including 102nd Indian Science Congress. More than 13 research papers and articles written by her on various issues have been published in reputed national/international journals. She has also contributed one chapter for an edited book. The teaching and research work of the author is focused on Special Education, Psychology and Mathematics. Email: meenakshi1801@gmail.com

**Dr. Nagendra Ambedkar Sole** is in the Department of Public Policy, Law and Governance and Dean, School of Social Sciences, Central University of Rajasthan. He was Formerly Director and Regional Director of Vardhman Mahaveer Open University, Kota, Rajasthan, and IGNOU respectively and has served as members in various bodies like Academic Council, Finance Committee, Research Council and Board of Management. One of his articles is suggested reading of Department of Public and International Affairs, George Mason University, U.S.A. He has published seven books and 21 articles in reputed journals and has successfully completed four projects. He has presented papers and chaired sessions of a number of National and International seminars and Conferences. He has 30 years of teaching experience and is also serving as National Vice President of New Public Administration Society. Email: snambedkar@curaj.ac.in

**Dr. Nalini Misra** is Assistant Professor in the Department of B.Ed., Khwaja Moinuddin Chishti Urdu, Arabi-Farsi University, Lucknow, (U.P.). Her qualifications are B.Sc., M.Sc. (Chemistry), B.Ed., M.Ed., UGC-NET (Education), Ph.D. Her areas of specialisation are Higher Education, Environmental Education and Guidance and Counselling. She has published articles in various national and international journals of repute. She has attended and participated in various national/international seminars and workshops.
Email: kuhoo2009@gmail.com

**Nidhi Singh** is a Research Scholar in the Department of Business Administration, University of Lucknow, pursuing her Ph.D. on topic "Impact of communication technologies on human development". She is NET-JRF in Management. Her keen interest area includes human development related concepts. Her publication includes one research paper in international journal. She has attended 9 national/international seminars and 3 workshops. Email: nidhiks7@gmail.com.

**Dr. Nutan Sharma** is an Assistant Professor in Sri Sai College of Education Badhani-Pathankot, Punjab with more than 10 years of teaching experience. He is Ph.D. in Education, NET in Education and Post-Graduate in Mathematics. His keen interest area includes Value Education, Philosophy, Teacher Education, Secondary Education, Teaching of Mathematics and Women Empowerment. He has attended more than 27 national and international seminars and conferences. He has published more than 30 research papers in national and international journals. He has guided more than 20 students at master level. Email: sharmassce@gmail.com.

**Palwinder Kaur,** is a Senior Research Fellow in Department of Education, Punjabi University, Patiala, Punjab. She is Post-graduate in Education, Political Science and has been awarded UGC-JRF in Education and Political Science. She is M.Phil. in Political Science. She has participated and presented papers in 13 national/international seminars and conferences. Three articles written by her on various issues have been published as seminar/conference proceedings and in national/international journals. Till now, she has contributed one chapter in distance education departmental notes of Panjabi University, Patiala, Punjab. She has also contributed one chapter in edited book. She had also worked as field investigator in State of Nation Survey—2008, 2009 conducted by *Lokniti* and sponsored by *CNN-IBN* and *The Indian Express*. She had worked as Assistant

Professor in Guru Tegh Bahadur College of Education, Malerkotla, Punjab. Email: kaurpalwinder999@gmail.com

**Dr. Rajeev Saxena** is an Assistant Professor in Department of Business Administration, University of Lucknow, (U.P.) with 16 years teaching experience and 12 years industry experience. He is post-graduate in Biotechnology and Management. He has done 'Selling Counsellor' training from Harvard Business School, U.S.A. He has research experience of 14 years. He has attended and presented papers in various national and international seminars and conferences. He has published more than 2 articles and research papers in various journals. Email: rajeevsaxena2008@yahoo.com

**Ratan Sarkar** is a Junior Research Fellow at Ramakrishna Mission Vivekananda University, Faculty of Disability Management and Special Education, Coimbatore, Tamil Nadu. He has B.A. (Honours) in English, B.Ed. in Special Education (MR), and M.Ed. in Special Education (MR). He has qualified NET in Education. He has presented 12 papers in national and international seminars/conferences and has 11 publications in journals, edited book, and other collections. His area of interests include teacher education, special education, inclusive education, assistive technology and devices, ICTs and its use in the inclusive setting for students with special needs, curriculum development for children with intellectual disabilities with a focus on critical pedagogy and cognition, empowerment of women, adapted games and sports, universal design for learning, vision of Swami Vivekananda on education, religion, and upliftment of marginalized groups. Email: ratansarkarju@gmail.com

**Dr. S. Parween** is an Assistant Professor at Faculty of Disability Management and Special Education, Ramakrishna Mission Vivekananda University, Coimbatore, Tamil Nadu. She has 15 years of experience in the field of Special Education including 6 years of teaching experience. She has qualified NET in Education in 2010. She has guided around 15 students at Master level. She has co-authored two books and published many articles in journals. Her areas of interest are Early Intervention, Assistive Technology and ICT for Persons with Disabilities, Emotional Intelligence, Soft Skill Development for the Visually Impaired, Inclusive Education, and Theatre Arts for Persons with Special Needs etc. Email: parweencbe@gmail.com

**Mrs. Shashi Bala** is Pursuing Doctorate in Botany, with 14 years teaching experience. At present she is working as Assistant Professor at SCD Government College, Ludhiana (Punjab). She is M.Ed. in

Education. Her keen interest involves Socio-political development of India and issues related to women and child. She has attended and presented papers in various national and international seminars and conferences. She has published more than 25 articles and research papers in various journals. Email: scd_sush@yahoo.in

**Ms. Shobhani Saxena** is an Assistant Professor in Monad University, Hapur, Uttar Pradesh with more than seven years teaching as well as industrial experience. She is pursuing Ph.D. in Mass Communication from NOIDA International University, NOIDA, (U.P.). She is M.Phil. in Mass Communication and Post-graduate and Graduate in Mass Communication. Her keen interest area includes Research, Women Empowerment, and Journalism. She has also worked as a News Anchor in Doordarshan Kendra, Bareilly (U.P.). She has published more than 100 articles in various newspapers. She has attended more than 13 national and international seminars and conferences. She has published five research papers in national and international journals. She has guided more than 22 students at PG level and 25 students at UG level. Email: active.shobhi@gmail.com

**Ms. Sneha Saha** is an Assistant Professor in Department of Psychology, National P.G. College, Lucknow (U.P.). She is awarded Gold Medal for her excellence in Masters of Psychology degree. She is pursuing her doctoral programme from Shri Ramswaroop Memorial University, Lucknow (U.P.). In a relatively new career span of three years in academia, she has been active with participation in conferences/seminars and workshops of national and international repute and publication of research papers. Her research papers have been in national and international journals. Her chapter has been published in book titled "Skills to Excel in Higher Education". She has successfully conducted a mini project titled "An Exploration of Academic Stressors and Stress Intervention Designs for School Students" with Kendriya Vidyalaya, Bareilly (U.P.). She has been invited as a resource person on many occasions for career sessions and personality development sessions. She works as a volunteer for number of NGOs for social causes. Her area of interest lies in the applications of psychology specificity to youth. She is a life time member to many reputable psychological associations of the country. Email: snehasaha1990@gmail.com

**Ms. Sushma** is presently working as an Assistant Professor at ICCMRT (Institute of Cooperative and Corporate Management Research and

Training) Lucknow (U.P.) a quasi-government body established by UP State Government. She has more than six years of teaching experience at Post-Graduate level. She is pursuing Ph.D. in management from Uttar Pradesh Technical University, Lucknow (U.P.). She is three times UGC-NET qualified. Her interest areas include Quantitative Research and Statistics with proficiency at use of SPSS. She has more than ten research papers published and has various National and International conferences participation. She has been a life member of ICA and SEDS. She has guided approximately 100 students at post-graduate level. Email: sush.87.06@gmail.com

**Dr. Vishakha Shukla** is Doctorate in Education, with five years of teaching experience. At present she is working as an Assistant Professor in Department of Education, Sampurnanand Sanskrit University, Varanasi (U.P.). She is post-graduate in Chemistry and Education. Her keen interest involves teacher education and guidance and counselling. She has written two books one on School Administration, Environment and Population Education and another on Guidance and Counselling. She has attended and presented papers in various national and international seminars and conferences. She has published more than 16 articles and research papers in various journals. She has contributed three chapters in edited book. Email: vishakhashukla17@gmail.com

**Zainab Farhat** is currently pursuing her Ph.D. from the Department of Public Policy, Law and Governance, Central University of Rajasthan. As an awardee of Maulana Azad National fellowship, her areas of interest are Minority Studies, Social Exclusion and Governance. Email: 2014phdpplg005@curaj.ac.in

# Introduction

This book entitled "Technology for Transforming Education—Emerging Trends and Issues" is a collection of 14 chapters contributed by eminent authors having vast teaching and research experience.

The first chapter of the book titled **Smart Classrooms: An Inclination Towards Integration of Technology in Education** authored by *Deepa Awasthi* has emphasised the use of smart classrooms to improve learning level of students. She has explained about the various tools and equipments, e.g. television, interactive white board, microphone with amplifier speakers, computer/laptop with internet connection, LCD projector, overhead projector, document camera, DVD player, concealed cable connectivity, inverter/UPS etc. commonly being used in creating a smart classroom. In her chapter author has detailed about the various advantages and disadvantages of smart classrooms and changed role of teachers in changed scenario. She has also mentioned the precautions necessary for teachers while handling a smart classroom. According to her appropriate training to prepare teachers for future is need of the hour so that, they can use smart classroom efficiently and effectively.

The next chapter titled **Multimedia and Teaching-Learning Process** authored by *Nutan Sharma* focuses on the role of multimedia technology in improving teaching-learning process and how it helps the teacher in achieving his or her goal in various ways. He has also highlighted the advantages and limitations of using multimedia in teaching-learning process. According to him use of multimedia is need of the hour in twenty-first century so that future citizens of tomorrow can learn their abilities and talents for development of country and make proper use of their education in real life to solve the upcoming problems. He also finds that use of multimedia is the tool to empower education; its use is not only beneficial to students but also to the teachers.

In the third chapter of the book titled **The Pedagogical Strength of Multimedia Technology in Education** authors *Mrs. Shashi Bala, Amitaraj Gargey* and *Amit Kashyap* focuses on the pedagogical strength and limitation of multimedia technology in the field of education. With the help of literature review authors have tried to explore how multimedia supported instructions affect the learners' performance related to presentation skill and effective writing. They have discussed the trends in instructional design in teaching how to use multimedia technology in changing learning environment. Multimedia technology activates multisensory organs—eyes, ears, brain etc. This multidirectional informational flow certainly accelerates the process of learning. Authors view that when teacher finds variety of learners in classroom then use of different media can be useful for them. Beside advantages, use of ICT and multimedia has certain limitations also. That is related to human information processing limitations. Authors have especially detailed about the increasing use of video clips and power point presentation in classroom for making teaching-learning process more effective and result oriented.

*S. Parween* and *Ratan Sarkar* in their next chapter titled **Inclusive Classrooms for Students with Disabilities—Role of Assistive Technology** focuses on the role of assistive technology to ensure and promote good quality education for the children with disability along with other normal children without disabilities in normal classroom to fulfil the objectives of Right to Education Act, 2010 to provide free and compulsory education to all the children of age group 6 to 14 years including CWSN. In the review authors find that there is need for the teachers to follow the principle of universal design of learning (UDL) to build inclusive classroom. According to authors achieving greater level of independence, confidence boost up, increasing participation in classroom, increased interaction with peers, increased access to teachers for problem solving, self-advocacy, seeking out new opportunities, are the few outcomes expected among CWSN through use of assistive technology in their day-to-day life. Authors have also discussed the various assistive technologies helpful for the students who are visually impaired, hearing impaired, mobility impaired, communicative disorder and learning disabilities etc.

The fifth chapter titled **Technology: A Facilitator for Learner Centred Education** authored by *Vishakha Shukla* focuses on the role of technology as facilitator for students centred education. According to her technology has affected the teaching-learning process to great extent in modern era. Development of basic skills among students increases with the use of technology in academics. With the help of 12 principles of student centred learning developed by Mccomb and Whistler in 1997—nature of learning process, goals of learning process, construction of knowledge, higher order thinking, motivational influences on learning, intrinsic motivation to learn, characteristics of motivation enhancing learning tasks, developmental constrain, social and cultural diversity, social acceptance, self-esteem and learning, individual differences in learning and cognitive filters can easily be applied on the issue of use of technology in teaching. She finds that in recent years great progress has been observed in introducing technology at all the level of education especially at higher level.

Next chapter of the book titled **Use of Technology in School Education: A Study of Selected Schools in Ajmer** authors *Zainab Farhut* and *Nagendra Ambedkar Sole* have focused on the practical aspects of use of technology in schools of Ajmer district of State of Rajasthan. They have visited three different types of school, e.g. Government school, affordable private school and missionary school. They compared the schools on the extent of availability of technology to students, competency of teachers to use the technology in classroom, interest of students in studying through use of technology and role of school administration and management in introducing use of technology in classroom. They have discussed the various challenges faced by stakeholders and strategies required to implement technology-based teaching methodology in classroom. Authors have utilized the World Bank Report 2010-2014, according to which Government of India has spent Rs. 2,585 crore in providing ICT infrastructure to schcol, yet by 2013-2014 only 60 per cent secondary schools are equipped with computers.

*Shobhani Saxena* in her chapter titled **Need of Introducing Technology Based Education in Rural India** views that under developed education sector is the main reason for low pace of rural development. Although Government of India has launched a number of programmes in field of education with various State Governments, at various levels to improve the current status of education in rural and other socio-economically backward areas, but the results achieved are much below expectation. She also finds that through use of appropriate technology; especially ICT the status of rural education can be enhanced. With the help of ISRO, Government of India has launched 'EDUSAT' for presenting educational videos to students of remote areas through web sources. Author finds that advance internet technology like Cloud Computing Module, Wikis, and Online media can be beneficial to teach rural students through interesting methods. She has also discussed the differences in traditional mode of teaching and modern innovative methods of teaching and its various implications. She also details how proper technological training especially computer training of rural youth may enhance their chances of better employment leading to rural development.

The eighth chapter titled **Tele-immersion in Education** authored by *Nalini Misra* has detailed a comparatively new concept known as Tele-immersion, which provide virtually real experience to user with the help of super computers and high speed internet. In future, Tele-immersion may replace video conferencing or tele-conferencing as it can create real, holistic three dimensional environment even when the two or more users involved in communication are physically separated. It creates a perception among users as they are standing in front of each other. She has detailed the full process how Tele-immersion works to create 3D image. Author also discusses the advantages and challenges associated with making the Tele-immersion technology, accessible to all. According to her Tele-immersion can bring revolution in the field of Education for addressing the problem of shortage of teachers, students sitting miles away can attend the lecture as real experience, even when educator is present in other city or even in other country. By this way technology-based on Tele-immersion can be a boon for formal education system as well as the distance education system.

In the next chapter titled **Perception of Academician towards Usage of Communication Technology** authors *Nidhi Singh* and *Rajeev Saxena* view that although use of communication technology is increasing day-by-day, but the techno-stress is affecting each and every mind at the same time. Use of technology *via* mobile phones has added new dimensions to it. According to KPMG report—2014 states that out of 6.8 billion people on earth, four million people are using mobile phone while tooth brush is used by 3.5 million people only. During literature review authors found that techno-stress is a modern disease dealing with inability to cope with new technology which have negative impact on attitude, thought and body physiology of the user. According to the experts techno-overload, techno-invasion, techno-complexity, techno-uncertainty and techno-insecurity are the five conditions which create techno-stress. Authors have conducted an exploratory research on academicians through self-structured open ended questionnaire-based on previous researches. Findings suggest that most of them use computers two to three hours daily and home and work place has no boundaries left for them. Their life is negatively affected by such development. Respondents also find that their dependency on technology has increased a lot extent. Authors suggest that there is need to establish a balance in use of technology, so that, personal life of individuals may not affected by its overuse.

Tenth chapter of the book titled **Developing Professional Identity: Technological Aid to Effective Teacher Training Programmes in Higher Education** authored by *Sneha Saha* focuses on the need of development of professional identity of teachers especially at higher education level with the help of use of technological aids at the time of teachers training programme. According to her the role of teachers in profession of teaching has changed to great extent from 'a person who teaches' to 'a person who guides' beyond the books. These changed roles have added new responsibilities to the duty of teachers, ultimately demanding for change in professional identity of teachers. She also finds that although educational institutes are progressing towards technological advancement *via* investing in various technological tools and instrument, but teachers training institutes are lagging behind in this process. She suggests that teachers must be encouraged to integrate technology in lesson plans, but this is only possible when they have easy access to computers, software, internet and other technical devices helpful in teaching-learning process. She feels that there is need to teach the teachers about how to use technology in classroom for making their teaching not only effective, but efficient also, this is also possible through appropriate pre-service and in-service training at regular intervals. Teachers must motivate to participate in online group discussion, forums, e-mail lists, bulletin boards, message boards and chat rooms along with regular traditional syllabus implemented in teacher training programmes.

The next chapter titled **Technological Integration with Teaching Pedagogy** authored by *Sushma* discusses how teacher can use technology in classroom for better understanding. She also tries to explore various relevant pedagogical issues needed to be addressed on priority basis for integrating with teaching. According to her teacher must understand the pedagogical principles governing the application of technology in teaching and learning. She has also explained the TPACK—Technological Pedagogical Knowledge Framework. Author has mentioned few critical areas needed to be evaluated, *i.e.* selection and adoption of technology suited to students need, choosing methods that are relevant to objectives, evaluation of technique selected, development of follow-up techniques, course enrichment, engaging, exciting interactive and energetic classroom etc. She further stresses on the role of teachers in decision-making about integration of technology in teaching-learning process.

*Meenakshi Dwevedi* in her chapter titled **E-Learning and its Impact on Teaching and Learning in Urban Age** discusses the concept of E-learning and its impact on teaching and learning. She has detailed about the various components involved in the process of E-learning. Author has differentiated the E-learning in to two categories—Synchronous and Asynchronous. She stresses on the need of blended learning as it provides an opportunity to learners to experience rich educational gain. She has listed the various benefits of E-learning and factors responsible for making E-learning more effective and popular among educators and learners. According to her personalized learning is best pedagogy for learners, in which pace of learning, instructional approach, lesson/content, activities and interest of learner are the key elements that are customized.

Thirteenth chapter of the book titled **Application of Multimedia Technology in Modern Teaching** authored by *Archana Jha* focuses on the use of multimedia technology in modern teaching-learning process. She has also explained the meaning and importance of multimedia technology for innovating and improving the teaching methods through individualization of instruction and developing an effective learning system. According to her multimedia approach and its tools are beneficial to students as well as to educators also. She has briefed the process of applying multimedia approach step-by-step; she finds that selection of appropriate media is most important step. Author believes that teachers can use the multimedia as an important tool for giving knowledge, removing misconception and doubts, raising the level of understanding and motivating the learners.

The last chapter of the book titled **Technology in Classroom: Benefits or Hindrance** authored by *Palwinder Kaur* has discussed the various advantages and disadvantages associated with use of technology in classroom for teaching students. According to her technology is advantageous as it promotes independent learning, easier access to information, promotes exciting ways to educate students, the information highway, broaden mindset, bring fun in classroom, helpful in profession, support collaborative skills, encourages engagement and motivation of students, provide current information and wider access, improves instructional delivery, support differential instruction, accomplishment of more complex task etc. Apart from this author has also mentioned the various disadvantages—laziness in study, forgetting the basic way of studying, searching for unusual and inappropriate content in computer through internet, disconnected youth, cyber bulling trap, inevitable cheating, distraction in studies, inadequate teaching methodology, wastage of time, unavoidable cost, incompatibility issues etc.

# 1

# Smart Classrooms

## An Inclination Towards Integration of Technology in Education

*Deepa Awasthi*

### Introduction

Classroom is the centre place for teaching and learning. Environment of classrooms decides the result of teaching. There is continuous effort from educationists and academicians to make the classrooms learner centred and interesting. The concept of smart classes is a stage in journey of development of field of education. The concept of Smart classroom is an advance technological implementation for schools which provides tools and contents for students learning, using latest media presentation. Smart classrooms are also known as digital classrooms or multimedia classrooms. They are electronically enhanced lecture classroom using computer and other multimedia network technology.

### Historical Background

In India Doon Public Schools, New Delhi were the first to use computer aided technology and learning through smart classrooms using plasma screen and smart assessment system (SAS) in all their classes. The Millennium Schools—an Educomp product were awarded as the best innovative K-12 school. Educomp is the largest

K-12 education company founded in India in 1994. At present more than 32000 schools and 20.9 million students are connected to Educomp all over the world. Apart from this, Pearson Education Company Pvt. Ltd., Tata Interactive, Next Education, E-learn India, HCL etc. are the other major players promoting the concept of smart classrooms in India. Little Millennium and Euro Kids chain of pre-schools is providing digital experiences to the kids at pre-primary level.

## Equipments and Tools Required to convert a Normal Classroom into Smart Classroom

There exists no defined set of standardised equipments and tools for smart classrooms. They may vary according to situation, content to be taught, teachers' compatibility with technology and level of learning etc. But for the sake of study some commonly used equipments are:

### *(a) Television*

Invention of television in nineteenth century has completely changed and superseded the all pre-existing communication technologies. It is very hard today to find a home without television. Initially, television was used purely for the purpose of disseminating information and entertainment but at later stages it was realised that television can also be used to promote education at great speed especially mass education. It is one of the most easy and acceptable source of education for learners. It evokes auditory as well as visual senses of learners.

Television is one of the most important tools to convert a normal classroom into smart classroom. Television can be more useful for the students at primary and pre-primary level, as teacher can play the pre-recorded CDs and VCDs with the help of VCD player. For example teacher wants the students to memorise the rhymes and poems, it is not possible for teacher to sing the rhyme, multiple times in classroom with appropriate action. He/she plays the poem on television and student learns the poem by listening and seeing with appropriate actions. With the help of television, teacher can create a virtual environment, *viz*. Forest, beach and mountains etc. (*See* Fig. 1.1).

*Source:* www.wisegreek.com

**Fig. 1.1:** Television Mounted on the walls of the Classroom

### *(b) Interactive White Board*

Interactive white board is a big touch sensitive screen with board acting as screen, mouse and keyboard at the same time. It can display the computer screen *via* connecting it to projector. It can be manipulated or instructed by use of hands/fingers or by specialized pen, it makes it easy to handle. Such type of interactive white boards can easily be used in giving demonstration, teaching through maps, storytelling etc. It is popular at all the levels (*See* Fig. 1.2).

### *(c) Microphones and Amplifier Speakers*

Microphones also known as 'Mic' is a instrument which is used to improve the sound quality by converting sound energy into electric energy and further electric energy into sound energy with the help of amplifier speaker. Set of microphone and amplifier speaker is especially useful in teaching the hearing impaired children (*See* Fig. 1.3).

*Source:* www.globalsources.com

**Fig. 1.2:** Interactive White Board

*Source:* www.amajon.in

**Fig. 1.3:** Picture of Microphone and Amplifier Speaker

### (d) Computer/Laptop with Internet connection

Computers with internet connection have changed each and every field of human life. Now, computer is important to human being as any other organ of body. They can be called as common key to all the locks. It can be used for instructing, guidance, testing, evaluation, library purpose etc. Its ability to connect to vast types of input devices such as key boards, mouse, scanners, microphones, joysticks, web camera, and digital camera etc. have made it so popular. Handling of computers is very easy, even the students of age 10 years can use the computers for their purpose. Its role in easing out the things has compelled us to give it so much importance in our daily life. In todays twenty-first century a individual who cannot handle the computers is considered almost illiterate.

*Source:* www.surfshocomputers.net

**Fig. 1.4:** Picture of Computer with CPU, Mouse and Keyboard

With the progress of time it was felt that professionals like Doctors, Engineers, Teachers or even individual engaged in clerical work cannot carryout his/her work efficiently without personal computer. This need led to the invention of Laptop, which were light in weight, easy to carry and technologically much advance. These new generation Laptop being carried on shoulder can do all the works which was only possible through permanently fixed computers with number of accessories attached to it making it more complex. For new generation youth Laptop has emerged as another body organ. There are continuous inventions going on to make it simpler and smaller, Tablets are now even replacing Laptops due to its smaller size. Ladies can easily keep these Tablets in their handbags.

*Source:* www.digimanindia.com

**Fig. 1.5:** Picture of Laptop

### (e) *LCD Projector*

LCD projector is a scientific device used to display video, image or computer data on screen or any other white surface. As name itself suggests LCD—liquid clear display, making it more and more popular not only in educational institutes, but also in offices. It can be connected with television, VCD player, Computer or laptop makes it easy to handle for purpose of presentation. They are portable in size and can be carried at place where required. During presentation size of display can also be adjusted as per the size of screen and requirement (*See* Fig. 1.6).

### (f) *Overhead Projector*

An overhead projector is variant of slide projector that is used to display images. The focusing lens of projector projects light rays on screen to produce real images. Printed or hand written transparencies are used as source to produce the images.

### (g) *Document Camera*

Document camera is able to magnify and project the images and three dimensional objects. It allows the teacher to present the printed sheet, map, book pages or any other display material on

*Source:* www.wisegreek.com

**Fig 1.6:** Picture of LCD Projector

*Source:* www.audio-ecolife.com

**Fig. 1.7:** Picture of Overhead Projector showing a Photograph on Screen

screen. High resolution camera takes the picture and produces a live picture using projector or computer. Some of the document cameras are so advance that they can even rotate at 360 degree to produce a three dimensional image. It is useful in classroom, presentation hall, training, video-conferencing etc.

*Source:* www.eu.hitachisolutions.com

**Fig. 1.8:** Picture of Document Camera

### (*h*) *DVD Player*

DVD player is a device that plays discs (DVD or CD) connected to television. It produces live picture and sound quality. They can be used to run audio CD. Although the role of DVD player can easily be played by Computers and Laptop, but all the laptops do not have DVD drive compulsorily. It can easily be connected to Projector. Twenty-first century DVD players are designed to use USB also (*See* Fig. 1.9).

### (*i*) *Concealed Cable Connectivity*

Although concealed cable networking does not play any role in teaching-learning process, but it is essential for running the smart classroom successfully. Concealed cable connectivity ensures safety of instrument as well as user. Conciliation of wiring prevents it from damages, e.g. fire, cut, rodents etc. Users also remain safe from electric shock. Concealed cable connectivity is helpful in getting rid of open bundle of wires (See Fig. 1.10).

### (*j*) *Inverter or UPS*

Inverter or UPS are important for smart classroom as they provide instant electricity backup to electronic equipments. In developing country like India continuous 24 hour power supply is still not guaranteed. Excluding the metro cities condition is much more horrible in small cities, town and other rural areas where

*Source:* www.k3dav.com

**Fig. 1.9:** Picture of DVD Player

*Source:* www.netfloorusa.com

**Fig. 1.10:** Picture of concealed wiring under floor

there is no fix time for power cuts. Computers and other electronic equipments are usually programmed in the way that abrupt power cut can destroy them, so Inverter or UPS attached to equipment provide enough opportunity to start electric generators or to close the systems in absence of power generators (*See* Fig. 1.11).

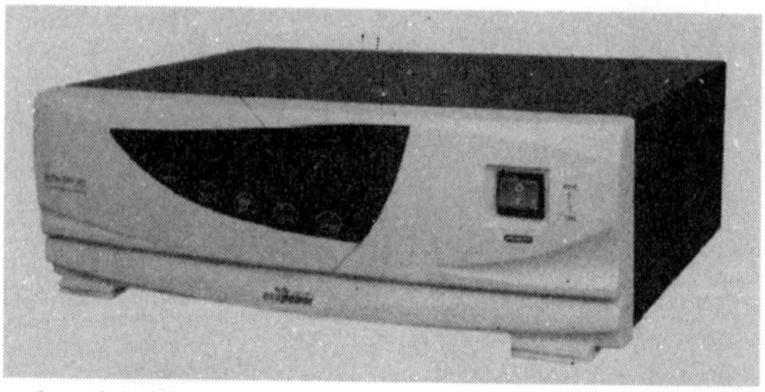

*Source:* www.dombiviliin.com

**Fig. 1.11:** Picture of Inverter

## Characteristics of Good Smart Classrooms

(1) ***It must be cost effective***: High cost of installation of smart classroom is still a concerning issue for school management in developing country like India. Ultimately, this increasing cost of education is directly or indirectly, is a burden on parents. In India school still lacks the basic minimum facilities like clean drinking water, clean toilets, boundary wall, appropriate seating facility etc., it is unjust on their part to expect them to make arrangement of smart classrooms.

(2) ***Equipment must be simple in use***: New technologies always bring difficulties for user. While selecting the tools for classroom, school management must make sure that they are simple in use. Equipments which are easy in handling make teacher's job easy. Complex equipments bring hesitation in minds of teachers and they may avoid or minimise the use of equipments.

(3) ***Must excite and attract students***: Equipments must be selected appropriately that they must excite and attract the students. It is necessary to engage and involve the students in classroom.

(4) ***It must reduce pressure from teachers***: Technology must be present in classroom to reduce pressure from teachers. Teachers must feel confidence with presence of technology.

(5) ***Equipments must be placed or fixed at appropriate place***: Smart classroom must be beneficial for all the students present in classroom. For this equipment must be placed at appropriate position, e.g. heights, so that, it can be easily viewed by the last benchers also.

## Advantages and Disadvantages of Smart Classrooms

Now, it is globally accepted that integration of technology in education enhances the learning abilities of students and modern days Smart Classrooms are the ideal examples of successful integration of technology in education in students' favour. Some of the advantages of creation of Smart Classrooms in schools are:

- *Helpful to Teachers in making the Teaching-Learning Easy*: The electronic technology used in smart classes usually helps the teachers to make the students more clear about the subject. Sometimes, teacher finds it difficult to make the students understand the difficult subjects like Science, Mathematics, Geography etc. in such a situation the technology can make teacher's job easy.
- *Availability of Wide Variety of Teaching Learning Material*: Wide use of Computer based technology and internet in smart classes enhance the reach of students to unlimited teaching-learning material available on-line. Knowledge level of teacher is limited and cannot be compared with the unlimited knowledge bank available on World Wide Web network. Sometimes, it is also found that knowledge of teacher is outdated and obsolete, because he has not been able to add new information to his knowledge bank, while on-line resources provide latest and updated information.
- *Involvement of Students*: Traditional classrooms were usually teacher centric or curriculum centric, where involvement of students was limited up to the role of listener only. But smart classrooms are based on student centric approach. Students not only search the new things, but they also create the knowledge.
- *Motivate the Students for Creative Thinking*: Usually, the teaching-learning process used to be boring and monotonous, where student use to listen the teacher and copy down the text and contents from blackboard. But the use of smart classrooms increases the motivation level of students. Use of technology evokes the interest of students in learning new things.

- *Promotes Collaborative and Cooperative Learning*: Use of smart classrooms in schools, promote collaborative action and cooperative learning among students. They come together to solve the new problems.
- *Helpful in Live Presentation*: Technology helps the teachers to present the content in better way. Students usually feel themselves completely connected due to the live nature of presentation.
- *Develops Problem Solving Ability*: Smart classes develop problem-solving ability among students. Technology gives them the chance to solve the virtual problems like real situation.
- *Helpful to change the perception of parents*: Optimum use of technology is helpful in changing the perception of parents. In this century when technology is affecting each and every field of life, parents feel confident that use of technology in teaching-learning process will ultimately prepare them for future challenges.
- *Useful for Children with Special Needs*: Various equipments used in smart classroom are useful to teach the children with special need.

Although there is common perception that use of Smart Classes is advantageous for learners and teachers, but that's not true. It has certain disadvantages also—

- *High Cost*: The cost of purchasing the equipments and electronic tools is too much. Ultimately, the cost is burdened on parents in the form of fee hike. Every parent cannot pay the fee on the name of smart classroom, which is five times higher as compared to fees taken by normal schools. Apart from purchase, maintenance of such equipments is also very costly. Most of the time school has to hire a permanent staff or involve in maintenance contract or both for such purpose.
- *Scarcity of Skilled faculty*: Due to continuous use of traditional teaching methods for prolonged period and absence of appropriate training infrastructure, developing countries like India and many others suffer from scarcity of skilled faculty that can meaningfully use the technology in classrooms.

- *Technical Failure of Electronic Equipments*: Electronic equipments used in classroom are delicate, and if not maintained and serviced properly from time-to-time, there are chances that they might not work when required.
- *Availability of Continuous Electricity Supply*: Electronic equipments usually run on electricity, for their smooth working of equipments a continuous supply of electricity on suggested voltage is required. In developing countries like India, where continuous supply of electricity is still a challenge, school has to manage high capacity electricity generators. It may further add to the cost of integrating technology with education.
- *Perception of Teachers*: Negative perception of teachers towards technology also acts as hindrance, especially old age teachers. They think that mostly students make misuse of technology and this misuse of technology distract their minds towards non-beneficial activities.
- *Lack of Appropriate Teachers Training*: Usually, during pre-job training teachers are trained to teach with traditional methods of teaching, then how can we expect a teacher to start teaching in smart classes with ultra modern technological equipments.
- *Every learner is different*: Every learner is different from others and same technology cannot be useful for every student sitting in classroom. For example an inclusive classroom where children with different special needs are sitting together need different technological instruments for their help. In such a situation, it is not practical or possible for teachers to get expertise of all technologies.
- *Government Policies*: Although Central and State Governments speak about the use of technology in schools, but there policy towards integration of technology in education can easily be understood when we find that for number of Government run primary as well secondary schools, television is still a dream.

## Changed Role of Teachers in Smart Classrooms

The wide use of technology in field of education has changed the role of teacher in classroom from 'instructor' or 'lecturer' to 'guide'. Initially, teachers use to sit or stand in front of students and use to instruct or deliver the lecture, but in smart classrooms teacher act as guide to help the students to learn and achieve the objectives. He/she minutely observes each and every student in classroom whether he/she is heading in right direction or not. He/she has to share background, content and skills rather than instructing them like a lecture delivering machine. He allows the students to explore the knowledge. Teacher interacts with students to share the knowledge, experiences and learning. He/she helps the students about how to learn and what to learn, remaining act is to be done by students themselves. They have to act as mediator between source of knowledge and learner.

## Precautions to be Taken by Teacher while Handling a Smart Classroom

Handling the smart classrooms is not easy for every teacher because usually all the objects used in smart classrooms are electronic equipments which are very delicate in nature. It requires a sense of responsibility and reliability on part of teacher. He/she has to take extra precaution while using electronic equipments and gadgets, but the precautionary attitude of teacher must not cross the limit as it is normally seen in Indian scenario. In India few schools have followed the concept of smart classrooms, but teacher still follow the traditional method of teaching as they are hesitant of using these equipments, due to the fear of getting damaged. In spite of this teacher should make full use of equipments with appropriate precautions—

- Teacher must ensure the regular maintenance and safeguards of equipments. Teacher must make sure that all equipments are closed properly at the end of classrooms. He/she must check that all electrical switches connected to equipments are on 'off' position.
- Teacher must make sure that standard procedure of turning 'on' and turning 'off' is followed strictly by themselves as well as by students. Usually, all these instructions are mentioned in instruction manual.
- It is responsibility of teacher to have an eye on the students

that they must not make misuse of tools like computers and internet etc.

- They must remain alert that electronic equipments are getting serviced and maintained from time-to-time from authorised service authority. It is also necessary that parts to be changed are original and genuine, duplicate parts may damage the apparatus.
- Most of the electronic equipments are highly sensitive to dust, so such type of equipments must be immediately covered after use. Proper dusting and cleaning will certainly add to the life of electronic equipments.

## Preparing the Teachers for Smart Classrooms

Teachers are the key element behind the success of any teaching methodology. If teachers can easily handle the equipments of smart classrooms, students feels better and parents are sure that precious time of their children will not be wasted. The big question arise whether the teachers in India are ready to take-up the challenge ahead, unfortunately the answer is no. It is unjust to expect a teacher to teach in smart classroom, when he/she has spent 25 to 30 years in teaching in front of blackboard through traditional teaching methods. Now, the point is what can be done to change the scene? Answer is advance level teacher training—pre-job training as well as in-job training.

Twenty-first century youth opting for teaching professional are already easy with technology. To make the pupil teachers well versed in utilizing technology for providing maximum benefits to learners, syllabus must be updated from time-to-time and latest information and global trends must be included to update the course content. In service teachers' training is much more serious issue, especially for government teachers. First of all government teachers are reluctant towards training, second existing corruption in system and government policy makes the in-service teachers training inefficient and ineffective. It is most important that teachers who are in service must learn the use of latest technique, a framework is immediately required which can motivate the teachers to learn and use the smart classroom in students favour.

## Suggestions to Promote Smart Classrooms in Schools

Although every stakeholder whether teacher, parents, school management, government, students are aware of the importance of smart classrooms, yet this concept has not developed at expected pace in India. The only reason to it is high cost and inability of financially week school management to bear the cost. But, it cannot be justified that due to this mere reason lakhs of students are excluded from its advantages. It is responsibility of government to come forward to implement smart classrooms in schools. For this they can provide subsidy or interest free loans to school management. Even corporate sectors spending crores of rupees in the name of CSR can come forward to help the schools.

## Conclusion

From above discussion we can conclude that concept of smart classrooms, although new to Indian education system is helpful in improving the teaching-learning process. In present scenario, all the stakeholders of education system—teachers, parents, school management and learners are hesitant to this technology integrated teaching-learning methodology due to different reasons. Government should come forward to promote smart classrooms in country and there could be no better place other than government run school-colleges, to demonstrate the advantages of teaching through smart classes.

## References

Chyn, Ong Shwu. *Advantages, Disadvantages and Challenges of Implementing Smart Schools*. Retrieved from www.slidesharre.net

*Computer in Education*, Retrieved from www.slideshare.net

Haridas, *Are Smart classes beneficial to students*? Retrieved from www.indiastudychannel.com

Jain, Seena. *Smart Classroom*, Retrieved from www.slideshare.com

LCD Projector, Retrieved from www.en.wikipedia.org

Poole, B. *Risks Involved in Integrating Technology in Classroom Teaching*. Retrieved from www.educationworld.com

Singh, K.D., *Computers in Education*. Retrieved from www.wikieducator.org

*Smart Classrooms—Advantages and Disadvantages*. Retrieved from www.targetstudy.com

*Smart Classrooms in Indian Education Scenario*, Retrieved from www.ukessays.com

*The Benefits of going for Smart Classrooms in your Education Institutes.* Retrieved from www.edtechboard.com

Wainwright, Ashley, *Ten Reasons Today's Student Need Technology in Classroom*. Retrieved from www.securedgenetworks.com

# 2

# Multimedia and Teaching

## Learning Process

*Nutan Sharma*

### Multimedia

Multimedia is in essence a presentation of information that incorporates multiple media such as text, audio, graphics, and animation. The representations can be redundant, incorporating the same content, or complementary, offering additional information. Multimedia need not be computerized, but computers offer some of the most seamless multimedia presentations. Moreover, digital multimedia, such as a simple CD-ROM, can offer teachers greater ease of presentation.

Multimedia *"provides a means to supplement a presenter's efforts to garner attention, increase retention, improve comprehension, and to bring an audience into agreement"*, which consequently results in people remembering 20 per cent of what they see, 40 per cent of what they see and hear, but about 75 per cent of what they see and hear and do simultaneously (Lindstrom, 1994).

Multimedia mirrors the way in which the human mind thinks, learns, and remembers by moving easily from words to images to sound, stopping along the way for interpretation, analysis, and in-depth exploration. The combination of media elements in a multimedia lesson enables trainees to learn more spontaneously and naturally, using whatever sensory modes they prefer. Combining media elements with well-designed, interactive exercises enable learners to extend their experience to discover on their own, so that they are no longer passive while information is "fed" to them. Instructional technologies help people learn to solve the problem and work as a team, which supports the development of interpersonal skills. With a multimedia programme trainers can provide more individualized attention to trainees as they need it most. Instructors have time to focus on activities that demand participation while students are able to learn on their own.

## Multimedia in Education

In the traditional education realm, the role of the teacher is to provide content and information to students. This can be done in the form of many instructional media, such as notes, diagrams, overhead transparencies, models and more. The information or content that is presented is based on the curriculum and other relevant information for the class. With technology, especially with multimedia authoring technology, the very same content can be converted into the electronic form and presented on the PC. The multimedia technologies used will transform the traditional materials into an interactive multimedia courseware.

With this transformation, multimedia is changing the way we communicate with each other. The way we send and receive messages is more effectively done and better comprehended. The inclusion of media elements reinforces the message and the delivery, which leads to a better learning and teaching environment. The power of multimedia lies in the fact that it is multi-sensory, stimulating the many senses of the audience, which consequently leads to better attention and retention rates. In other words, multimedia provides "an individual or a small group using a computer to interact with information that is represented in several media, by repeatedly selecting what to see and hear next" (Agnew, Kellerman and Meyer, 1996).

The education field is in the process of change driven by the new developments in technology; such developments determine the relationship between technology and education (Salinas, 1997). Educational institutions are adapting their teaching and learning processes to the technological advances (Cabero & Salinas, 2000). In addition, such advances are providing revolutionary tools like Web pages and multimedia-interactive systems. These tools can be integrated as a new way to teach (Bartolomé, 1998). There are following values of multimedia in educational process:

1. Multimedia approach can convey vast information and provide many sources from which students can get access to the information.
2. Through multimedia approach a large number of models of learning can be practiced over a great range of content.
3. Multimedia approach provides the opportunity to gain mastery of competencies and skills which are based on theoretical knowledge.
4. Multimedia approach is not restricted to a single type of learning style or instructional mode. It can provide the support of a wide range of activities.

It is a teaching process that uses multimedia in the presentation of instructional material, often in a way that requires the student to interact with it. When teacher uses multimedia in her class, it is said to use multimedia approach to teaching. In Multimedia approach, the teaching-learning process is carried out through a number of media by using them in such a planned and organized combination with reference to the available teaching-learning situation that leads to their utmost utilization for achieving the desired ends in a quite effective way.

## Use of Multimedia Applications in Teaching-Learning Process

Multimedia is playing a significant role in today's era. The biggest advantage of multimedia is, it makes students to express and represent their prior knowledge and provides them with many learning opportunities. Multimedia brings forth students' talent in various ways. It empowers students to work as a designer while designing their slides, browsing and interpreting the information and then representing their knowledge to others. There are following uses of multimedia in the teaching-learning process:

### *1. To Highlight Teaching Points*

With the help of multimedia the teaching points can be highlighted properly so that students can retain these for further use. Rational use of multimedia can effectively compensate for the lack of traditional teaching. The content or hard to understand things are not easy to see the full display but with the help of media to help students can understand the concepts or principles.

### 2. *To Strengthen the Interaction between Teachers and Students*

Multimedia courseware helps the students and teachers to reflect interactive relationship. The interactive features can enhance the sense of participation of students and improve learning initiative. It stimulates students' interest and curiosity, and promotes the comprehensive development of the quality of students. Effective use of modern teaching media has expressive, controlled, participatory techniques, on the one hand information in various forms of teaching to students, guide students to actively participate, on the other hand to the students with sufficient thinking and display space, and make timely responses to the evaluation of students, feedback to students, for students to control their own learning activities.

### 3. *To Facilitate Experiential Learning*

Multimedia technology offers the opportunity to simulate reality and therefore can facilitate experiential learning. Through video and sound, a real-life scenario can be conveyed and then the interactive and non-linear access capabilities of multimedia can enable the student to explore the situation as if for real. The student makes decisions and can see the consequences of those decisions. These capabilities of multimedia technology mean that it can be used for the application of previously learned concepts, or for a more inductive approach to learning.

### 4. *To Improve Learning*

In order to assess the effectiveness of multimedia courseware in the learning process we must first define the educational objectives which higher education seeks to achieve. Educational objectives can be broadly classified into subject-specific objectives and more general transferable skills. The limitations of multimedia in terms of its ability to promote the achievement of the above objectives must be recognized by the designers and users of the technology.

### 5. To Improve Quality of Teaching

Use of multimedia teaching methods, teacher can accelerate the speed and reduce the difficulty of teaching materials, better understanding of the depth of material. When we use media in our classrooms, the quality of instruction can be improved as the maximum senses of the students involved during the lecture. Large amount of information transmission speed is one of the characteristics of multimedia teaching, which can greatly improve the unit of time the number of students to acquire knowledge to enable students in schools have learned to constantly adapt to the needs of social development.

### 6. To Improve Teaching and Learning Environment

With the use of multimedia projector, or slide the inefficient duplication of media can be avoided such as writing on the blackboard, audio, video and other audio-visual media.

### 7. Flexible

Multimedia courseware or CD-ROM can be used at work on the desktop or at a learning centre, at home, while travelling, or to enhance facilitated management development programmes. Multimedia courseware can also be used on networks, intranets or Internet. These distributed learning approaches allow for even more flexibility, but in the cases of Internets will involve much lower quality images and will preclude the use of video, at least in the near future. Multimedia courseware off loads repetitive training tasks and frees facilitators to focus on company-specific, department-specific, or even team-specific issues.

### 8. Practical Approach

It is capable of presenting true-to-life situations that learners face everyday. Adults are very practical learners they learn best when faced with real problems that have real consequences. Decision tree simulation, video simulations or simple animations allow learners to learn-by-viewing, learn-by-doing or learn-by-coaching. All are effective methods for developing practical skill and increasing information retention.

### 9. To Remove Traditional Approach

The use of multimedia teaching tools, allows the people to change the traditional teaching philosophy gradually. It puts heavy emphasis on education and learning; attention from the simple transfer of knowledge, to both the importance of knowledge to impart, and also to capacity-building. The use of multimedia computer management teaching, teaching management can be more scientific.

### 10. Multiple Learning Channels

One of the key benefits of multimedia methods of teaching in both school and work settings is the increase in available channels for teaching. Some students learn better through visuals, some students learn better by listening, and some learn by working through material on their own. Multimedia aspects of on-line teaching allow teachers and trainers to use all the three methods, reaching students more easily no matter their learning type.

## Challenges

In present scenario we are facing a time of information evolution, in the ever-changing world our teachers and students require the right to information from the right sources. The present world is changing rapidly and the field of education is also experiencing these changes in particular as it applies to media services. The old days of an educational institution having an isolated audio-visual department are long gone! The growth in use of multimedia within the education sector has accelerated in recent years, and looks set for continued expansion in the future. Teachers primarily require access to learning resources, which can support concept development by learners in a variety of ways to meet individual learning needs. The development of multimedia technologies for learning offers new ways in which learning can take place in schools and the home. Enabling teachers to have access to multimedia learning resources, which support constructive concept development, allows the teacher to focus more on being a facilitator of learning while working with individual students. Extending the use of multimedia learning resources to the home represents an educational opportunity with the potential to improve student learning.

Besides benefits of multimedia in teaching-learning process there are some of the limitations as well as suggestions follows:

- The challenge confronting our educational systems is how to transform the curriculum and teaching-learning process to provide students with the skills to function effectively in this dynamic, information-rich, and continuously changing environment.
- Multimedia should be viewed as a support to learning and not as a substitute for good teaching or a teacher.
- Powerful computers are required to handle sound, images, animation and videos. Fast broadband is also needed for Web applications. These resources can be costly.
- Computer literacy is required for both teachers and students to use multimedia resources. Hence, it is essential that practical knowledge should be given to them so that they can utilize their skills to use computers effectively in the classrooms.
- Professional development is required for teachers to become confident in using multimedia and in finding existing resources. So, there should be proper provision of seminars, workshops etc. Pre-service and in-service training both are complimentary so proper training should be provided.
- Money, time and skills are needed to produce multimedia resources, such as a short instructional videos or programmes. Time is required to select suitable multimedia resources that are relevant, of high quality and have educational value.
- Health issues with students spending long hours in front of a computer need to be considered.
- The professional development of teacher educators is also essential. Unless teacher educators make effective use of technology in their own classes, it will not be possible to prepare a new generation of teachers who effectively use the new tools for learning.
- Multimedia is not the solution to all the educational challenges. Rather, it is an emerging technology that can

be developed in an effective or ineffective fashion. To create an appropriate approach we should become familiar with its potential. Technology by itself will not solve educational problems; rather the intelligent and creative development of a multimedia approach may provide an alternative method.

## Conclusion

Educational gains can be maximized when the most appropriate tools are used. However, it is not possible to give recipes for what technology tools to use or when to use them. Each case is distinct. But we can try to identify situations where the use of certain instructional multimedia material regularly achieves success. In such cases, it is also important to keep in mind the infrastructure or pedagogical constraints that may impede effective use of such multimedia. We focus on the use of video, sound, simulation, and animation, and explore considerations that affect their development. Multimedia technology is becoming increasingly popular in education as a means to motivate students in their learning and to provide them many ways to express their ideas and display their information. It also allows the teacher the flexibility to present their curriculum in an innovative manner. The application of multimedia technology into classroom instruction innovates on outdated teaching methods and techniques confined within the conventional one-way directed pedagogical model of teacher cramming and student passively spoon-fed instruction.

It promotes interactivity between instructors and learners, encouraging and enhancing students' engagement in the learning process. The major features of interactivity and being real-time provider and encouraging environments for students to learn with greater interest, initiative and creativity, and thereby remarkably improve classroom instruction effectiveness as well as the mutual development of teachers and students. Hence, it is the need of twenty-first century to use multimedia in the teaching-learning process so that our future generations could use their abilities and talents in the development of the country and make proper use of its advantages in their real life to solve the problems. Thus, for the purpose to improve the quality of teaching, we should combine the multimedia and other advanced teaching methods in the multimedia teaching models with those advantages in the traditional teaching, so as to enable them to provide a better service for the teaching objectives.

## References


Bartolome, A. (1998). Los Ordenadores en la Enseñanza están cambiando, *Comunicacióny pedagogía: Nuevas tecnologías y recursos didácticos,* 154: 22-28.

Cabero, J., and Salinas, J. (2000). *Nuevas Tecnologías aplicadas a la Educación,* Madrid, España.

Hofstetter, F.T. (1995). *Multimedia Literacy,* McGraw-Hill, U.S.A. www.imej.wfu.edu

Jensen, R.E. and Sandlin, P. (1991). *Why do it? Advantages and dangers of new ways of computer-aided teaching/instruction.* San Antonio, TX: Department of Business Administration, Trinity University.

Kellerman, A.S., and Meyer, J. (1996). *Multimedia in the Classroom,* Allyn & Bacon, Boston.

Lindstrom, R. (1994). *The Business Week Guide to Multimedia Presentations: Create Dynamic Presentations That Inspire.* McGraw-Hill, New York.

Mangal, S.K. and Mangal, Uma (2009), *Essentials of Educational Technology,* PHI Learning Pvt. Ltd., New Delhi.

Neo, M. and Neo, T.K. (2000), Multimedia Learning: Using multimedia as a platform for instruction and learning in higher education, *Proceedings of the Multimedia University International Symposium on Information and Communication Technologies* 2000 (*M2USIC'*2000), P.J. Hilton, October 5-6: S3-1.1-1.4.

Nitin, G. (2012). Benefits of Multimedia in Education: An Innovative Model, *Online International Interdisciplinary Research Journal, (Bi-Monthly),* 2(6): 239-247.

Oblinger, D. (1991). Introduction to Multimedia in Instruction. Maximizing Multimedia: A how to session for faculty, //unpublished manuscript distributed during training, Dallas Country Community College District at Dallas. Courtesy of PBS Adult Learning Satellite Service.

Zuras, M. (2010). *Teach art history.* Part 2. Retrieved from www.switched.com

# 3

# The Pedagogical Strength of Multimedia Technology in Education

*Shashi Bala, Amitaraj Gargey* and *Amit Kashyap*

*"If we teach today as we taught yesterday, we rob our children of tomorrow."* —**John Dewey**

The development of modern educational technology, especially the rapid development of the information superhighway as well as the emergence of multimedia computer technology, has a significant impact on education. Use of multimedia in instruction is the main component of modernization of instruction, as well as the breakthrough of overall instructional reform. Integration of multimedia in teaching can promote the reform of instructional modes and teaching contents. Multimedia technology is becoming increasingly popular in the field of education. Interactive multimedia courseware is adding a new and interesting dimension to both teaching and learning. This new approach can effectively complement the conventional methods of teaching and learning. The multi-sensory input of this media provides possibilities for higher performance ratings and higher retention. With effective feedback, this method makes learning and teaching more meaningful. Students with different learning abilities can work at their own place, time and pace. A significant aspect of multimedia in education is related to developing multimedia. Multimedia authoring as a form of computing has made it possible for students and teachers to construct knowledge and discover worlds which do not exist in conventional methods of learning or teaching. Above all, this new experience has defined a new concept of 'Edutainment'—a combination of education and entertainment.

As a new type of teaching methods, it can make teachers impart knowledge to the students in the most natural and receptive form of multimedia instead of the traditional blackboard and chalk and dry theory sermon. This kind of teaching method not only extends the amount of information that people receive and makes learning more interesting, but also increases the learning initiative and scientific accuracy. Therefore, education is one of the application fields that multimedia technology can maximize its power and influence. It demonstrates its charm to people in a new teaching model. Roger Murphy from Visual Learning Lab, University of Nottingham has rightly said, "Extensive research shows that visual imagery can play a powerful role in accelerating learning. Complicated concepts and processes can often be conveyed much more simply in a visual format, and evidence suggests that use of visual media can enhance problem-solving, motivation, understanding and the expression of ideas."

## Changes in the Learning Environment and Multimedia

In order to gain insight into the changing learning environment and how multimedia is affecting learning, some discussion about trends in instructional design should be considered. Traditionally, learning was relied on a textbook and lecture format for the transfer of knowledge.

The student was a passive recipient of knowledge under this format. Traditional schooling treats learning like a savings bank where knowledge is deposited for future use (Papert, 1993). Much of this knowledge remains inert, and meaning is not accessed even though it is relevant for problem-solving. When knowledge is acquired through a problem-solving mode, instead of a factual mode, the information learned is less likely to remain inert (Hasselbring, 1994). Students must understand why, when, and how various skills and concepts are relevant or the knowledge will not be used. Students need the ability to think independently. They should be able to identify and define problems and develop strategies for solving these problems on their own rather than simply responding to the problems posed by others. One way to help students become independent thinkers is to anchor instruction in meaningful problem-solving environments (Hasselbring, 1994). Examples of problem-solving environments include scenarios, case studies, hands-on projects etc. Providing students with meaningful problems to solve makes the students; more active participants in the learning environment. Students can see the implications of their new knowledge and learn the appropriate conditions to apply this knowledge. Providing students with a context-rich, problem-solving environment can increase learning and retention. Computers, especially computer-based multimedia systems can provide problem-rich environments that help students learn.

## Need of Multimedia Technology in Education

Besides being a powerful tool for making presentations, multimedia offers unique advantages in the field of education. With multimedia, the process of learning becomes more goals oriented, more participatory, and flexible in time and space, unaffected by distances and tailored to individual learning styles, and increased collaboration between teachers and students. Multimedia makes learning friendly and fun-oriented without fear of inadequacies or failure.

The pedagogical strength of multimedia is its natural information-processing abilities that we already possess as humans. Our eyes and ears, in conjunction with our brain, form a formidable system for transforming meaningless sense data into information. The old saying—"a picture is worth a thousand words" often understates the case especially with regard to moving images, as our eyes are highly adapted by evolution to detecting and interpreting movement. For example, a photograph of Ganges in Varanasi, apart from being aesthetically pleasing, can contain a wealth of information relating to the culture, religion, geography, geology, climate, history, and economics of the area. Similarly, a recording of a politician's speech can allow us to discern significant semantic features not obvious in a written transcript.

Moreover, teachers' now-a-days realize that in education 'learning' is more important than teaching. Learning is concerned with pupils whereas teaching is concerned with pupils and teacher.

In the olden days, teacher was the only source of knowledge. The students learnt what the teacher taught. With the advent of text books and other learning aids, the teacher's personal knowledge though important, ceased to be the only or even the paramount source of learning. Various multimedia aids such as radio programmer, the film-producer and many others now assist in the learning process.

The science of teachers' behaviour is called 'pedagogy' and that of pupils' behaviour is known as 'mathetics'. Now, emphasis is laid on mathetic principles in contrast to pedagogical principles. Learning is given more importance than teaching and mathetic principles are used for devising programmes, developing methods and curricula. The educational universe should not be 'teacher centred', but 'pupil centred' and stress is not so much on 'what' as it is on 'how'. Keeping in mind the shift from pedagogy to mathetic the teacher has to restructure the environment for effective learning and utilize educational technology in an integrated manner. Educational technology seeks to integrate the relevant principle of psychology, sociology, linguistics, communication and other allied fields. It attempts to incorporate the principles of management like resource development, system analysis and cost effectiveness.

Secondly, the traditional classroom with one teacher teaching 30 to 40 students which was mainly one way communication of information is no longer effective in the present educational world. The two general factors—'information explosion' and 'population explosion' are bringing changes in the developed and developing countries. Both of them have posed critical problems for education more things to be learnt and more individuals to learn. It is not possible to solve them by conventional means. For solving these problems successfully, multimedia technology is required. Especially in developing countries like India it has to be mastered and utilized by educationists, if they are to keep pace with each other and catch-up with developed nations. As such, both quantitative expansion as well as qualitative improvement of education can be facilitated and accelerated with the help of multimedia technology.

## Advantages of Multimedia

When we incorporate multiple media into an application, more of our senses are activated. Consequently, one reason to use multimedia is to give life to that information. Multimedia encourages users to embrace, internalize, and lean more from information because users can attain the information from multiple directions. In other words, users of multimedia applications have an opportunity to read about information, and to see it, hear it, and watch it move. Today, most web based multimedia applications consist primarily of elements that involve our eyes and ears, but this, too, is changing. Smell and touch are beginning to have place in web based multimedia applications.

Each of us learns differently and each of us is inspired by something different. When we use multimedia, we are able to tap into these differences. For example, some people have visual personality. They learn or are inspired by reading, seeing, or visualizing. Other people are auditory and learn best by listening. Finally, there are kinaesthetic learners who learn by doing.

Although each of us has a preferred learning style, for all of us, our learning experience is enhanced when each learning style is accommodated. In fact research shows that people remember only 20 per cent of what they see and 30 per cent of what they hear. When people see it and hear it, they remember 50 per cent (Computer Technology Research, 1993). When people see it, hear it, and interact with it, they remember 80 per cent. That is big difference, which certainly supports the tremendous growth of multimedia and justifies its use.

Apart from this, students respond to information differently. Thus, it is often to our advantage as teachers to use many different formats and modes to teach the subject matter of a lesson. This is why teachers normally use some combination of lecture, text and hands-on laboratory for conveying information.

With the advent of the Internet and the multiple formats that can be communicated over the World Wide Web, we now have several new and exciting ways to present information. The Web allows the incorporation of animation, moving pictures, and sound into lessons, which extends our abilities to present materials that encourage student interaction with the subject matter. Pictures and animations help bring to life scientific principles, and multimedia allows students to take a more active role in learning: they can watch experiments in action, and use a mouse or keyboard to navigate images, simulations and interactive material.

One major advantage of interactive multimedia systems is the degree of learner control. Learner controlled instruction allows the student to study material at a pace that suits his/her needs. Students are under less pressure to perform within certain time limits. Learners can choose a logical route through the instructional material that is meaningful to them. Multimedia instructional systems allow learners the opportunity to explore material of their choice at a pace which is comfortable to them. Students are more interested in the material since they choose the pace and the sequence of the content. This increases the relevance of the material and creates a greater desire to learn, which in turn helps to increase knowledge retention.

Considerable research has shown that students learn more effectively when the instruction is consistent with their cognitive style (Gagne, 1985). Multimedia enables the learner to organize the information in a manner that reflects his learning style, thereby improving the retention and retrieval of knowledge (Norman, Genter, Steven, 1976). The way students review multimedia instructional material mirrors the way they think, learn, and remember. Students move between text, images and sound, stopping for a time to interpret, analyze, and explore. Multimedia adapts well to individual differences due to the high degree of learner control and the ability to map too many learning styles.

**Limitations of Multimedia**

Potential disadvantages of multimedia should be taken into account to avoid pitfalls when using multimedia for instructional purpose. Major problem with multimedia systems is related to human information processing limitations. While multimedia can provide engaging displays, bombarding the learner with too much information can lead to cognitive overload. If the learner's attention is divided among too many sources, learning will likely not occur. It is important to maintain the learner's interest but a careful balance must be kept to avert confusion. To avoid cognitive overload, the number of user choices (links to other areas of the programme) should be kept within the guideline. Media types should be used to help convey information not simply to impress the user with technology. Proper use of colour, font size, logical grouping, and location coding can lower the complexity of the system leaving more cognitive resources available for learning.

**Selected Studies**

The use of video clips as a teaching tool in courses has increased in recent years. The benefits of effectively utilizing video clips in courses are significant and appear far ranging, and evaluations from both students and instructors have been favourable. Although opportunities exist across a wide variety of courses for successful integration of this medium, courses in interpersonal communication seem particularly conducive. Specifically, video clips have been integrated into the curriculum to display functions of voice quality, silence, cross-cultural, and eye communication.

However, in spite of the putative merits of video in professional communication classroom, there is little empirical data and research to measure the efficacy of video as an instructional tool for improving professional communication skills of the students. With regard to video technology, lack of systematic and organized approaches in integrating this type of educational media in schools is very apparent. As argued by Rhodes and Pufahl (2011), there are a small number of officially evaluated video based programmes. Furthermore, a body of literature (Ortiz *et al.*, 2012; Wagener, 2006; White *et al.*, 2000 etc.) shows that investigation and in-depth analysis of the advantages of the instructional use of video technology is in its initial phase. The literature also suggests that the integration of video in classroom activities only at an elementary level with arbitrary selection of teaching methods may diminish a full extent of learning effectiveness.

For instance, two studies carried out by Ortiz *et al.* (2012) and Wagener (2006) clearly indicate a strong necessity for more empirical research in this area. As such, English language teachers have relatively limited insights into scientific explanations of the educational potential and benefits of utilizing video technology in classroom settings. Moreover, the effect that use of instructional video has on presentation skills development, the major body of previous studies relied on self-reported and descriptive information provided by the learners. Few focused on its direct impact on learners' achievement in terms of presentation skills development. Therefore, the objective of the present study is to examine whether the inclusion of instructional' videos serves to enhance the presentation skills of the learners.

Like other instructional aids the use of PowerPoint in the classroom appears to be embraced enthusiastically by faculty and administrators at institutions nationwide. Faculty members are contributing countless hours in the preparation of slide show presentations to accompany lecture material. Textbook companies are contracting with individuals to construct textbook specific slide shows in an effort to increase the marketability of their textbooks. While the use of PowerPoint and multimedia in the classroom has significantly increased all-around the world in recent years (Connor and Wong, 2004; Bartsch and Cobern, 2003), few studies have systematically investigated its impact on student learning.

The research regarding the impact of lecturing with PowerPoint on academic performance has been mixed as some researchers have found that it enhances students' academic performance (Mantei, 2000; Szabo & Hastings, 2000) whereas others have found no effect (Daniels, 1999; Rankin & Hoaas, 2001). Previous research either lacked a comparison of PowerPoint lectures to traditional lectures or students compared the instructor PowerPoint lectures to traditional lectures in other courses.

## Conclusion

From the review of literature in reference with a variety of university approaches, it has been learnt that multimedia has enormous potential to impart flexible, multi-modal, lifelong education to heterogeneous mass learners. The Multidisciplinary nature of multimedia makes it increasingly popular among people from diverse domains. The literature study clearly demonstrates its qualifications as a vast source of customized learning environments, to accommodate varied behavioural problems like confidence building and stress reduction. Multimedia used in right direction has also succeeded in psychomotor development and strengthening of visual processing of the intended users.

In conjunction with the study of usefulness of multimedia in different educational scenarios, the important point for future research is that the time to come will surely promise the availability of multimedia technology to one and all, but its usage should be limited to and in consideration with its pedagogical strengths. The above studies have clearly indicated that even if the networked classroom technology is made available to the students, there were many other pedagogical issues because of which the students' interest and interaction in the classroom could not be increased. More research work is required in the area of multimedia pedagogy so that the design, form and content of Multimedia is such that it does not hinder the usual educational process and supplements it with more info-edutainment.

> *"Technology can become the "wings" that will allow the educational world to fly farther and faster than ever before—if we will allow it."*
> ***—Jenny Arledge***

## References

Bartsch, R.A., and K.M. Cobern (2003). "Effectiveness of PowerPoint Presentation in Lectures," *Computers and Education,* 41.1 : 77-86.

Connor, M., and Irene F.H. Wong. (2012). "Working through PowerPoint: A Global Prism for Local Reflections," *Business Communication Quarterly,* 67.2 (2004): 228-231.Web. 2 November.

Cuban, L. (1993). *How Teachers Taught.* New York: Teachers College Press.

Daniels, L. (1999). "Introducing Technology in the Classroom: PowerPoint as a First Step." *Journal of Computing in Higher Education,* 10.2 : 42-56. Web. 15 January, 2013.

Gagne, R.M. (2012). *The Conditions of Learning.* New York: Holt. 1985. Google Books. Web. 4 March.

Goodlad, J. (1984). *A Place Called School.* New York: McGraw-Hill Book Company.

Hake, R. (1998). "Interactive Engagement *versus* Traditional Methods: A Six Thousand Students Survey of Mechanics Test Data for Introductory Physics Courses." *American Association of Physics Teachers.* 64-74.

Hasselbring, T.S. (1994). "Using Media for Developing Mental Models and Anchoring Instruction." *American Annals of the Deaf,* 13.9: 36-44.

Malik, S. (2012). "Use of Multimedia as a New Educational Technology Tool—A Study", *International Journal of Information and Education Technology,* Vol. 2, No. 5, October.

Mantei, E.J. (2013). "Using Internet Class Notes and PowerPoint in the Physical Geology Lecture", *Journal of College Science Teaching,* 29 (2000): 301-305. Web. 14 June.

Moore, M.G. and Kearsley, G. (1996). *Distance Education: A Systems View.* New York: Wadsworth.

Norman, D.A., (1976). Gentner, D.R., and Stevens, A.L. "Schemata and Memory Representation." *Cognition and Instruction.* Ed. D. Klahr. Hillsdale, N.J.: Lawrence Erlbaum Associates.

Ortiz, J., Burlingame, C., Onuegbulem, C., Yoshikawa, K. and Rojas, E. (2012). "The Use of Video Self-Modelling with English Language Learners: Implications for Success." *Psychology in the Schools,* 49.1: 23-29.

Rankin, E.L., and Hoaas, D.J. (2001). "The Use of PowerPoint and Student Performance," *Atlantic Economic Journal,* 29 : 113. Web. 11 May, 2010.

Rhodes, N., and Pufahl, I. (2011). *Language by Video: An Overview of Foreign Language Instructional Videos for Children,* Washington, DC: Centre for Applied Linguistics and Delta Publishing Company. *Google Books*. Web. 25 March, 2012.

Seymour, Papert (1994). *The Children's Machine: Rethinking School in the Age of the Computer*. New York: Basic Books.

Sungu, S., and Tekkaya, C. (2006). "Effects of Problem based Learning and Traditional Instructions on Self-Regulated Learning", *The Journal of Educational Research*. 99: 307-317.

Szabo, A., and Hastings, N. (2000). "Using IT in the undergraduate classroom: should we replace the blackboard with PowerPoint?" *Computers and Education,* 35: 175-187.

Vyas, Poonam (2013). *A Comparative Study of Traditional and Multimedia Supported Techniques for Imparting Communication Skills at the Tertiary Level,* Birla Institute of Technology and Science Pilani (Rajasthan) India.

Wagener, D. (2006). "Promoting Independent Learning Skills Using Video on Digital Language Laboratories," *Computer Assisted Language Learning,* 19.5: 279-286.

White, C., Easton, P. and Anderson, C. (2000). "Students' Perceived Value of Video in a Multimedia Language Course," *Educational Media International,* 37.3: 167-175.Web. 13 March, 2013.

# 4

# Inclusive Classrooms for Students with Disabilities

## Role of Assistive Technology

*S. Parween* and *Ratan Sarkar*

### Introduction

More than one billion people in the world live with some form of disability, of whom nearly 200 million experience considerable difficulties in functioning. In the years ahead, disability will be an even greater concern because its prevalence is on the rise (WHO, 2011). According to Census of India (2011), 1.5 per cent of the total population is school going children with disabilities in India. The paradigm shift from exclusion to inclusion of persons with disabilities occurred after the enactment of the landmark legislation United Nations Convention on the Rights of Persons with Disabilities (UNCRPD) which promotes including children with disabilities in educational systems.

Inclusive education is a kind of education in which children with disabilities are placed in regular education classrooms with children of the same age who do not have disabilities. The underlying premise of inclusion is that all children can learn and belong to the mainstream of school and community life. The task of providing equal educational opportunities to the under privileged disabled community would be made possible only through making inclusive learning environments with adaptations in the infrastructural and instructional aspects to meet the unique needs of diverse learners.

The fundamental notion of Inclusive Education is that school must recognize and respond to the diverse needs of their students, accommodating both different styles and rates of learning and ensuring quality education to all through appropriate curriculum, organizational arrangements, teaching strategies, resource use and partnership with their communities (Lipsky & Gartner, 1999).

Assistive Technology or Adaptive Technology (AT) is an umbrella term that includes assistive, adaptive, and rehabilitative devices for people with disabilities and also includes the process used in selecting, locating, and using them. AT promotes greater independence by enabling people to perform tasks that they were formerly unable to accomplish, or had great difficulty accomplishing, by providing enhancements to or changed methods of interacting with the technology needed to accomplish such tasks.

The effectiveness of using assistive technology and devices with students who have difficulties to foster academic success and independence is stressed in many researches (Olson, Foltz & Wise, 1986; Higgins, MacArthur, Schwartz & Graham, 1991; Bryant, Smith & Carter, 1997; Bryant & Seay, 1998). It was also found that Assistive Technology and devices are not only used in remediation; such devices may also provide a compensatory alternative that circumvents deficits while capitalizing on an individual's strengths (Garner & Campbell, 1987; McGregor & Pachuski, 1996; Bryant & Bryant, 1998).

Technology can be the great equalizer in a classroom with diverse learners. The definition of Assistive Technology applied to education is extremely broad, encompassing "any item, piece of equipment, or product system whether acquired commercially off the shelf, modified, or customized, that is used to increase, maintain, or improve functional capabilities of individuals with disabilities."

A number of Assistive Technology devices and software are available that, with careful planning and guidance, can benefit students with disabilities (Duhaney & Duhaney, 2000). "Assistive Technology" can often help teachers personalize lessons and skills enhancement to each child. Most students with disabilities can and do benefit from technology in the classroom. Incorporating technology increases students' motivation to learn and personalizes lessons to a student's individual needs. Even the students with the most severe and profound disabilities can use Assistive Technology to join a classroom of typical students, and their potential can be reached in ways we did not have before.

Researches indicate that Assistive Technology has had a positive impact on students' learning (Kober, 1991; Sivin-Kachala & Bialo, 1993). Studies also reveal that it is how teachers adapt and utilize the technology that makes a difference and not the technology itself. The effect of Assistive Technology on student with disabilities were positive, reaching that potential requires knowledge on the part of the user (Merbler, Azar, & Ulman, 1999). There are four considerations when matching students with disabilities to assistive technology. The first consideration is to assess the student and know his/her capabilities and limitations. The second consideration is to know what is available in assistive technology. The challenge is to match the two for a successful learning experience. The third consideration is the ease of use of a device, the learning curve for the user or by standers, and the noise level of the device. The fourth consideration is to match the Assistive Technology tool to age, gender, preferences of the user to promote acceptance and use (King, 1999).

Studies show the following outcomes among students with disabilities who regularly use Assistive Technologies:

- Achieve greater levels of independence;
- Gain confidence;
- More participation in classroom activities;
- Increased interaction with peers;
- Increased ability to reach teachers for clarifications;
- Self-advocate;
- Challenge themselves; and
- Seek out new opportunities.

Despite the increased attention to and awareness of the potential of AT to help individuals with disabilities access the general curriculum and acquire transitional skills, as reflected in the federal legislation, several barriers remain. First, despite the existing educational technology (Zhang, 2000), accessible technology is unavailable to many students with disabilities and their families. For example, Norman (1994) observed that not all groups have equal access, primarily due to limited financial resources. Second, the high, costs of equipment and lack of funding to access devices or services, as well as lack of information regarding AT for families of individuals with disabilities, are often primary barriers (Wehmeyer, 1998). Third, professionals, lack of knowledge about technology can be a major obstacle. For example, few training programmes for special education teachers include courses or class sessions on AT applications and issues (Todis, 1996). Fourth, lack of ongoing support can constitute a main problem. Fifth, eligibility issues are often important obstacles, and have led to the underutilization of AT by individuals with disabilities (Wehmeyer, 1998).

Use of Assistive Technology in the classroom helps not only the students with disabilities, but the teachers also use it during curriculum transaction which facilitates teachers' interaction in the inclusive classrooms. Assistive technology can provide a teacher more options to use in addressing different learning styles for individual students using visual, auditory and tactile approaches. By making a student more independent, Assistive Technology allows teachers to spend more time on group activities and to give students more one-on-one attention. The variety of available AT tools has grown rapidly in recent years. Students use this assistive technological devices based on their specific needs.

## Assistive Technology for the Students with Visual Impairment

The technology for the visually impaired (fully or partially) may be able to help them in the classroom, workplace, or the management of their home. In the educational context the children with visual impairment will be able to make use of Printed Text Resources such as Braille Books and Tactile Graphics. With the use of Braille Printing Machines and Braille Embossers, the text materials are made available to the blind children in Braille format. The invent of sophisticated machines such as Three Dimensional (3D) Laser Printers, Thermal Heaters—ZyFuse, Sparsh Tactile etc., reduces the burden of the classroom teachers. These machines produce tactually explorable high quality pictures, diagrams and maps that are present in the mathematics, science and social science text books.

For those who are not trained to read and write Braille, the Audio/Talking Books could be helpful. Computer software—Windows Media Player, VLC, WinAmp, CD/ DVD recorders and Players can help the students to access the text material as audio-outputs. The availability of Digital Talking Books (Digital Access Information System—DAISY) facilitates the reading process by navigating the written material which is otherwise impossible through conventional recorders and players.

The learners who have reading disabilities including blindness, impaired vision, dyslexia or other issues can access E-Text Resources through Screen Reading Software (Non-Visual Desktop Access NVDA, Job Access with Speech JAWS, SuperNova, Windows Eye, SaySo, SeroTalk, Voice, ORCA etc.). The other devices for the visually impaired would include:

- Magnifiers (Book Magnifiers, Pocket Magnifier, Handheld Digital Magnifiers, Screen Magnifiers—*Distance View, Clear View*).
- Refreshable Braille Displays (Focus, Seika, ALVA, Brailliant, Tactile Displayers).
- Braille Note Takers (Braille Note, Seika Mini, PACMate, BrailleSense).
- Independent Scan and Read Devices (SARA, Read EasyMove, Clear Reader, La Voice Solo, Blaze Reader).
- Smart Canes.
- Large monitors.
- Adjustable task lamp using a fluorescent bulb shines directly onto the paper and can be adjusted to suit.
- Bank note reader.
- Copyholder holds printed material in near vertical position for easier reading and can be adjusted to suit.
- Closed circuit television (CCTV) or video magnifiers. Printed materials and objects are placed under a camera and the magnified image is displayed onto a screen.
- Spell checkers and Grammar checkers.
- Coin detectors.

## Assistive Technology for the Students with Hearing Impairment

Following are the various assistive technologies which can help to solve the problems of students with hearing impairment in school as well as in day-to-day life:

- The classroom amplification devices were used initially for the amplification of teachers' voice in the classroom. There are different types of classroom amplification devices. Hard-Wire System was the first group amplification system developed for the benefit of the education of the hearing impaired. Induction loop amplification systems were developed in order to permit mobility of the teacher and the child in the classroom while still achieving high quality amplification.
- Infrared Systems and Frequency Modulated (FM) System are other amplification devices that could be used for students with varying degrees of hearing loss.
- Assistive listening devices (ALDs) are designed to reduce the effects of distance, background noise and reverberation. The ALDs reach out and grab the desired sound and send it directly to the listener's ears minus the deleterious effects of distance, background noise, or poor room acoustics. The converser pro-multi-pack can be an ideal solution for use in school classrooms to improve the quality of sound we hear.
- Signal enhancement systems provide enhanced listening in conjunction with personal hearing aids or may be substituted for the hearing aid in specific listening situation.
- Signal assistive devices convey verbal communication information by means other than the acoustic signal.
- Signal alerting devices alert persons to sounds that otherwise might be inaudible or not loud enough to attract attention.
- Auditory aids are those that facilitate optimal use of residual hearing by the hearing impaired individual. There are a number of such aids available, for example, personal hearing aids of all types, group amplification systems and speech trainers.

Out of all the available systems of amplification for use with the hard of hearing, the individual hearing aids have greater general amplification value. The auditory trainers and group hearing aids differ only in the degree to which we are able to modify and control amplification, the modality with which they provide the individual and the specific value of the talk for which the system is designed. They are much larger than the individual aids and moderately portable.

## Assistive Technology for the Students with Communication Disorders

Life is all about communicating and interacting with one's environment. Assistive technology offers a chance for active participation for those having issues in communication. The benefits that assistive technologies have for individuals with communication disorders are enormous. Not only the impact of being included in a regular classroom environment will be felt, but also being included in life is now a reality.

An inclusive environment promotes interactions of various kinds for all individuals. Augmentative and Alternative Communication (AAC) is the umbrella term used to describe the full range of communication methods that can be used to supplement or substitute for 'normal' speech or writing for those with impairments or restrictions on the production or comprehension of spoken or written language. AAC could be any method that supplements or replaces speech and writing when these are temporarily or permanently impaired and inadequate to meet all or some of a person's communication needs. The term encompasses everything from gestures and signing, to aids, which can be low-tech (such as picture boards) or high-tech (employing the latest technology). Impaired communication or speech loss can result from a range of conditions, including Down's syndrome, autistic spectrum disorders (ASD), acquired brain injury, cerebral palsies, hearing impairment and learning disability.

Communication aids under AAC are usually categorised into two broad groups: unaided and aided, with the aids subdivided into low-tech and high-tech. Low-tech communication aids are defined as those that do not need batteries, electricity or electronics to meet the user's communication needs. These are often very simple aids created by placing letters, words, phrases, pictures and/or symbols on a board or in a book, which may be accessed depending on physical abilities and limitations, users might indicate the appropriate message with a body part, a head or mouth stick or light pointer. Alternatively, they might indicate yes or no as a listener scans through the possible options.

High tech AAC aids are electronic devices that permit the storage and retrieval of messages, with most allowing the user to communicate with others using speech output. Such devices can also be referred to as Speech Generating Devices (SGDs) or Voice Output Communication Aids (VOCAs). Quick Talker and GoTalk Pocket are recently found in the market to benefit students with communication problems.

Access to AAC entails a complex interrelationship between the features of the AAC technology, the individual's physical abilities (e.g. motor, sensory, perceptual, cognitive and linguistic skills), and the device users' and their communication partner's abilities to interact. Technological development in direct selection and scanning has dramatically increased access to AAC technologies for individuals with a wide range of communications needs. Some people with severe communication impairments can use their hands to use AAC; others who cannot do so use alternatives such as mouth sticks, head sticks, switches or eye pointing.

## Assistive Technology for the Students with Mobility Impairments

The commonly used assistive devices by individuals with mobility impairments are discussed as under:

- Wheel chairs, Standing wheelchair, Electric-powered wheelchair (EPW), are designed to be a replacement for walking. For users who cannot manage a manual joystick, head switches, chin operated joysticks, sip-and-puff or other specialist controls may allow independent operation of the wheelchair.
- A mobility scooter is a motorized assist device similar to an EPW, but with a steering 'tiller' or bar instead of the joystick, and fewer medical support options.
- A Power-assisted wheelchair is a recent development that uses the frame and seating of a typical manual chair while

replacing the standard rear wheels with wheels that have small battery-powered motors in the hubs.

- Crutches (Forearm, Underarm, Stutters and Platform types) are mobility aids used to counter mobility impairment or an injury that limits walking ability.
- Walking sticks (canes) serve an identical purpose to crutches, but are held only in the hand and have a limited load bearing capability because of this.
- A walker or walking frame is a tool for disabled who need additional support to maintain balance or stability while walking. Modern walkers are height adjustable and should be set at a height that is comfortable for the user, but will allow the user to maintain a slight bend in their arms.
- Rollators are typically more sophisticated than conventional walkers with wheels. They are adjustable in height and are equipped with a seat and sometimes with a basket; with the use of modern materials, they are light-weight yet sturdier.

**Assistive Technology for the Students with Learning Disabilities**

Assistive Technology can offer powerful tools to students with learning disabilities by providing remedial or compensatory support in the classroom and for independent learning. Learning disabilities are professionally diagnosed difficulties with reading, writing, speaking, listening, spelling, reasoning or math. It can reduce a student's reliance on parents, siblings, friends and teachers, helping the transition into adulthood and fostering self-esteem and reducing anxiety. The below mentioned assistive tools support the students with learning disabilities in carrying out various functions:

**Tools for Writing**

- Scholastic Keys
- Graphic organizers and outlining
- Computer software-pen friend, Active words
- Abbreviation expanders
- Writing grips-Adapted paper (e.g., raised surfaces, highlighted lines, various colours, sizes

- Talking spell checkers and electronic dictionaries
- Word-prediction programmes
- Abbreviation expanders.

**Tools for Reading**

- Voice recognizers
- Predictive Word Processor
- Spell check software
- Reading windows
- Reading pens
- Audio books
- Speech synthesizers/screen readers
- Books on tape
- Highlighters

**Tools for Listening**

- Velcro, softball as reminders
- Recorders
- Handy-cassette
- Variable speed tape recorders

**Tools for Organization and Memory**

- Memo pads
- Reminders
- Self-sticking notes
- Information/data managers
- Time management calendars
- Watch reminders

**Tools for Calculations (Maths)**

- Talking Calculators
- Electronic math worksheet
- Table grids

## Conclusion

The role of assistive technology is imperative in the holistic rehabilitation of the children with disabilities. Such technologies not only help students better understand concepts and keep up with their peers, they also allow the school to better and more easily integrate students with disabilities into general education classes. Thus, mainstreaming of assistive technologies is having a significant impact on students. Although assistive technology has the potential to act as an equalizer by freeing many students from their disabilities, the barriers of inadequate awareness, availability, training and cost must first be overcome before more widespread use can become a reality. No doubt, Government of India has taken numbers of initiatives to implement inclusive set-up, but still a long path is remaining to be travelled. Though the principles and guidelines of universal design of learning are already put into practice, but still much work is need to be done to ensure the availability and accessibility of technological devices for students with disabilities for successful inclusion.

## References

Bryant, B.R., Seay, P.C. (1998). Technology-Related Assistance to Individuals with Disabilities Act: Relevance to individuals with learning disabilities and their advocates. *Journal of Learning Disabilities,* 31: 4-15.

Bryant, D.P., and Bryant, B.R. (1998). Using assistive technology to include students with learning disabilities in cooperative learning activities. *Journal of Learning Disabilities,* 31: 41-54.

Bryant, D.P., Smith, R., and Carter, A. (1997, October). The effects of computer-based instructional practice *versus* teacher-mediated paced error drill on math facts fluency of students with learning disabilities. Paper presented at the Council for Learning Disabilities International Conference, Washington, DC.

Duhaney, L.M., and Duhaney, D.C. (2000). Assistive technology: Meeting the needs of learners with disabilities. *International Journal of Instructional Media,* 27(4): 393-402.

Elkind, J. (1993). Using computer-based readers to improve reading comprehension of students with dyslexia. *Annals of Dyslexia,* 43: 238-259.

Garner, J., and Campbell, P. (1987). Technology for persons with severe disabilities: Practical and ethical considerations. *The Journal of Special Education,* 21: 24-32.

King, T.W. (1999). *Assistive Technology: Essential Human Factors.* Allyn & Bacon: Boston.

Kober, N. (1991). *What we know about Mathematics Teaching and Learning.* Washington, D.C.: Council for Educational Development and Research.

Lipsky, D.K. and Gartner, A. (1999) "Inclusive education: a requirement of a democratic society" in Daniels, H. and Garner, P. (eds.) *World Yearbook of Education* 1999: *Inclusive Education.* London: Kogan Page.

MacArthur, C.A., Schwartz, S.S., and Graham, S. (1991). A model for writing instruction: Integrating word processing and strategy instruction into a process approach to writing. *Learning Disabilities Research and Practice,* 6: 130-136.

McGregor, G., and Pachuski, P. (1996). Assistive technology in schools: Are teachers, ready, able, and supported? *Journal of Special Education Technology,* 13: 4-15.

Merbler, J.B., Hadadian, A., and Ulman, J. (1999). Using assistive technology in the inclusive classroom. *Preventing School Failure,* 43 (3): 113-118.

Norman, K.L. (1994). Spatial visualization: A gateway to computer-based technology. *Journal of Special Education Technology,* 12: 195-205.

Olson, R., Foltz, G., and Wise, B. (1986). Reading instruction and remediation with the aid of computer speech. *Behavior Research Methods, Instruments, and Computers,* 18: 93-99.

Sivin-Kachala, J., Bialo, E.R. (1993). *The Report on the Effectiveness of Technology in Schools 1990-1992.* Washington, D.C.: Software Publishers Association.

Todis, B.J. (1996). Tools for the task? Perspectives on assistive technology in education settings. *Journal of Special Education Technology,* 13: 49-61.

Wehmeyer, M.L. (1998). National survey of the Use of assistive technology by adults with mental retardation. *Mental Retardation,* 36: 44-51.

Zhang, Y. (2000). Technology and the writing skills of students with learning disabilities. *Journal of Research on Computing in Education,* 32(4): 467-479.

# 5

# Technology: A Facilitator for Learner Centred Education

*Vishakha Shukla*

## Learner Centred Education

The learner centred education reflects the necessity of centralization on both learners and learning. Several features characterize student-centred learning. Students have opportunities and increased responsibility to identify their own learning needs, locate learning resources, and construct their own knowledge based on their needs rather than having a standard or identical knowledge base imparted or given to all students. Technology acts as a facilitator for the learning, where students are at the centre of own learning.

## Principle of Student Centred Learning

McCombs and Whisler (1997) developed 12 major principles of student-centred learning that are—

(1) The nature of the learning process,
(2) Goals of the learning process,
(3) The construction of knowledge,
(4) Higher-order thinking,

(5) Motivational influences on learning,
(6) Intrinsic motivation to learn,
(7) Characteristics of motivation-enhancing learning tasks,
(8) Developmental constraints and opportunities,
(9) Social and cultural diversity,
(10) Social acceptance, self-esteem, and learning,
(11) Individual differences in learning, and
(12) Cognitive filters.

**1. *The Nature of the Learning Process and Use of Technology*:** McCombs and Whisler (1997) defined the learning process as a natural one of pursuing personally meaningful goals. This process is active, volitional, and internally mediated. It is a process of discovering and constructing meaning from information and experience, filtered through each learner's unique perceptions, thoughts, and feelings. Learning becomes an active process, in which the student is constantly engaged in a task. Being so involved, the student seeks his/her own underlying meaning. One of the goals of active learning is to have the classroom activities focused on reasoning and the evaluation of evidence.

The two characteristics of the learning process, are *Active Involvement* and *Direct Experience*. *Active Involvement* speaks about students' engagement in their learning tasks. Active learning is anything that involves students in doing things and thinking about the things they are doing. *Direct Experience* relates to learner-centred learning because learning is more effective when the students experience it directly.

The above mentioned characterization of learning can be enhanced exponentially by the use of technology in teaching-learning process. For example in flipped classroom concept students watch lecture videos as homework and discussion is carried out in the classroom in class time by the teachers. It has resulted in a remarkably better student performance with noticeable grade boost-up. Student can learn at their own pace and save class time for interaction. Thus, with the help of technology children learn according to the nature of learning process.

**2. *Goals of the Learning Process and Technology use*:** McCombs and Whisler (1997) stated that "the learner seeks to create meaningful, coherent representations of knowledge regardless of the quantity and quality of data available." To accommodate the goals of the learning process, the concept of *making meaning* is one of the most persistently honoured goals of teaching. By focusing on in-depth understanding, the quality of learning is greatly enhanced. Teachers are more likely to see what students do know and understand. That is why teachers employ different strategies to develop students' understanding. They strive to come up with clear explanations and open-ended tasks that call for and build understanding. Now-a-days we are emphasizing on social constructivist approach. Social constructivist teachers help their students to understand that they are co-constructors of knowledge and can make sense of things themselves.

For example teachers can collaborate to share their ideas and resources on-line. They can communicate with others across the world in an instant, meet the shortcomings of their work, refine it and provide their students with the best. This definitely enhances the practice of teaching.

3. ***The Construction of Knowledge and Technology*:** This concept means that the learner links new information with existing and future-oriented knowledge in unique and meaningful ways. It also means that students need opportunities to do more than just receive information. They need to confront new challenges using their past experience without the dominance of a teacher/ giver of information. *Patterns* and *Connections*, a sub-element of the Principles of Learning section, is also related to the construction of knowledge. Patterns and Connections mean that students are asked to examine the information they are studying, find relationships and build understanding based on them. The activities concerned with this domain can be brought by use of programmed activities, the observable behaviours are flexible thinking where student is able to adapt to new learning contexts and tasks by connecting, organizing and acting on previous skills and knowledge to new ones. Critical thinking involves task comparing, refining, and selecting from what he knows to find the best solution of the problem. Another behaviour is transfer, in backward reaching transfer he makes connections to previous knowledge and in forward reaching transfer he learns how to use the information in future. Sense making where in a specific learning context student is able to use familiar patterns that are re-organized and extrapolated so that they become meaningful in new situation.

Examples of use of technology is programmed learning, programmed instruction and podcasts and vodcasts which provide students with opportunity to learn at their own pace and freedom to go back and relearn the content whenever they want thus providing flexibility and adaptability to differentiated learning.

**4. *Higher Order Thinking*:** This represents the higher order strategies for "overseeing and monitoring mental operations, facilitating creative and critical thinking and the development of expertise" (McCombs & Whistler, 1997). Educational reformers wish to teach students how to ask questions, build their own interpretation and ideas, clarify and elaborate upon the ideas of others. *Empowerment* is one major element that focuses on how to empower students when they confront difficult situations. It looks at how to help them develop the thinking skills to make conjectures about what the problem is and how best to approach it.

*Power Sharing* is a very important feature of today's education because sharing various interpretations of a material adds an extra dimension in the learning process as students not only learn how others perceive a certain issue, but also appreciate the various reasoning processes and life experiences that support different interpretations.

This active involvement of students in learning also addresses the idea of *Decision-Making*; they need to possess the ability to critically, creatively and reflectively make decisions. Through *Critical Thinking* learning involves not merely the acquisition of information, but also the development of critical skills for evaluating facts and the interpretation of facts.

*Thinking Together* in problem-solving groups means that one student works on the problem while the others ask questions about what is being done. They help each other develop a plan for the symbolic support of their thinking. Above activities can be performed by the use of multiple computers. It enables the use of more interactive educational tools which allows for a dynamic learning experience that directly benefits the students.

**5. *Motivational Influences on Learning and Technology*:** These influences reflect the importance of learner beliefs, values, interests, and goals, expectations for success, and emotional states of mind in producing either positive or negative motivations to learn.

The motivation to learn has four dimensions: behavioural, humanistic, cognitive, and socio-cultural. Behavioural motivation is expressed through rein forcers, rewards, incentives, and punishers. From a humanistic point of view, the motivation to learn is characterized by a need for self-esteem, self-fulfilment, and self-determination. The socio-cultural motivation to learn is realized through engaged participation in learning communities and by maintaining identity through participation in activities of a group. By the use of technology students can develop valuable research skills. Technology gives students immediate access to an abundance of quality information which leads to learning at much quicker rate. They get connected with other students and teachers, share information and get motivated, know their culture. They get immediate feedback by programmed learning.

**6. *Intrinsic Motivation to Learn and Technology*:** Intrinsic motivation to learn refers to the fact that individuals are naturally curious and enjoy learning, but intense negative cognitions and emotions (e.g. feeling insecure, worrying about failure, being self-consciousness or shy, and fearing corporal punishment, ridicule, or stigmatizing labels) thwart this enthusiasm.

Creating classrooms that foster the continuing impulse to learn begins with seeing learning through children's eyes. To promote students' readiness to learn, social constructivist teachers are likely to focus their efforts on helping their students find their passions, discover what they care about, create their own learning agendas, and most importantly, connect to what they do in schools. Technology helps to overcome the negative cognitions and emotion by individualized learning and enhances their intrinsic motivation to learn.

**7. *Characteristics of Motivation-enhancing Learning Tasks*:** These include curiosity, creativity, and higher order thinking, which are stimulated by relevant, authentic learning tasks of optimal difficulty and novelty for each student. Curiosity is a skill that enables the learner to follow a hunch, question alternatives, ponder outcomes, and wonder about options in a given situation. Such situations can be brought about by the use of technology. Online learning now-a-days provides students with variable tasks of their interest. It provides access for face-to-face interaction. There are plenty of resourceful and credible websites available on internet that both teachers and students utilize.

**8. *Developmental Constraints, Opportunities and Technology*:** This refers to how individuals progress through stages of physical, intellectual, emotional, and social development that are a function of unique genetic and environmental factors. These factors make each individual different because students possess different kinds of minds and therefore learn, remember, perform, and understand in different ways. Learning through use of technology is now an equally credible option, face-to-face interaction is huge, especially in the younger years, but some students work better when they can go at their own pace. Self-learning overcomes developmental constraints.

**9. *Social and Cultural Diversity*:** Learning is facilitated by social interactions and communication with others in flexible, diverse (in age, culture, family background, etc.), and adaptive instructional settings. To stress the idea of social and cultural diversity, it requires the ideas of *Civil Involvement with Others, Communication,* and *Tolerance* to emphasize the importance of developing students' interpersonal skills and interactions.

*Communication* involves the relationships between student and student or between the teacher and the students. Communication involves the cooperation of those who work in a democratic society. Schooling is one context for learning how to live in a democratic society. *Tolerance* is the element which shows that children need to be friendly, cooperative, approving, affectionate, and willing to share. Children in a democratic society need to develop compassion, cooperation, and the ability to accept responsibility for their actions.

*Civil Involvement with Others,* focuses on an important strategy, which is to help the children create a collective identity, a sense of themselves as a group rather than a collection of individuals. The purpose is to foster social bonding; that is, to help children perceive their connections to one another.

Technology use is centred primarily on collaboration and sharing, web computer application encourages student's self-expression, interaction with peers and opportunity for authentic learning experiences. By the use of internet, on-line libraries, teleconferencing, watching on-line videos of different cultures, reading about great personalities of various cultures, their sayings, slogans etc. children develop respect for other cultures, tolerance is generated in them for others and they get also involved in various activities of their interest by means of internet.

**10. *Social Acceptance, Self-esteem, and Learning through Technology*:** Learning and self-esteem are heightened when individuals are in respectful and caring relationships with others who see their potential, genuinely appreciate their unique talents, and accept them as individuals. Social acceptance fosters interactive instruction because in a social setting, skilled thinkers model critical and creative thinking, thereby exposing novices to what is normally invisible. Thus, the teachers have multiple opportunities to move students towards critical and creative thought by the use of internet, on-line learning.

In interactive setting learners receive feedback on their ideas, conclusions, judgements, and so on. Feedback can help refine their ability to think critically and creatively. Frequent feedback provides opportunities for students to practice what they have previously learned. Individualized instructional programmes by the use of technology gives feedback to the student step-by-step.

**11. *Individual differences in Learning and Technology*:** Learners have different capabilities and preferences for learning modes and strategies. These differences are a function of environment (what is learned and communicated in different cultures or social groups) and heredity (what occurs naturally as a function of genes). The *Student Characteristics* deals with students' multiple intelligences and Dunn's Learning Style Model, which shows that students are different from one another, and thus, they reason and learn in different ways. Thus to satisfy their individual needs individualized instructional models are developed so that they can learn at their own pace and according to their own interest. Personalized system of instruction (PSI) is an important example.

**12. *Cognitive Filters and Technology*:** These consist of personal beliefs, thoughts, and understandings that result from prior learning and interpretations. They become the individual's basis for constructing reality and interpreting life experiences. To construct their reality, learners must spend the larger part of their time with activities that ask them to do thought-provoking tasks such as explaining, making generalizations, and, ultimately, applying their understanding on their own. And they must do these things in a thoughtful way, with appropriate feedback to help them do better.

Thought provoking tasks in form of software have been developed so that students can practice and get the immediate feedback.

## Students at the Centre of their Own Learning and Technology

As our world becomes more technologically advanced, schools need to understand and anticipate the changes produced by technology and its impact on how students learn. From elementary schools to college campuses, computers have been incorporated into the educational programmes, enabling students to have more freedom, flexibility, and individuality in the classroom. In addition, computers provide an opportunity for independent exploration, for personalized training, and for the opportunity to learn cooperatively.

Technology is not hardware or software. It is the powerful tool that learners can use to facilitate their own learning process. Teachers can use technology resources to provide opportunities for learning and create the conditions that optimize learning. Technology provides the means for the teacher to re-examine the nature of the classroom environment. The teacher is no longer the fount of all knowledge. Technology can provide access to sources beyond the classroom and the textbooks. The teacher can become the facilitator of learning, incorporating a host of strategies to guide learners. Technology opens the door to the world, allowing learners to access libraries, other learners and experts, and a vast array of resources to obtain the knowledge they seek.

Technology can be used to develop information processing skills and dispositions. Databases, simulations and access to the Internet can provide rich experiences and information as students acquire the skills and knowledge represented by the content standards. Students can also practice the tenets of democracy while engaging in technology mediated activities.

## Advantages of Technology

Technology facilitates the quality education. Students are becoming increasingly digitally literate. Technology use is particularly important in STEM fields. STEM is an acronym for science, technology, engineering and mathematics. Technology use in STEM has implications for workforce development, national security concerns and immigration policy.

- With the use of computer technology in classroom setting students are now able to have new authentic and meaningful experiences.
- Another advantage of using technology in classroom is its flexibility and adaptability to differentiated learning technologies such as podcasts and vodcasts which provide students with the opportunity to learn at their own pace and the freedom to go back and relearn content whenever they want.
- Technology helps in storage of information which enables students to learn anywhere and anytime.
- Quick data processing, audio-visual aids, better presentation of information, access to internet, quick communication among students, teachers and parents.
- It provides a mechanism for transparent collaboration between dispersed computer groups, enables the operation of large scale application, provides access to distributed resources from our computer.
- Technology use captures audience attention and arose their interest, it highlights main points of message clearly, here possibilities of misinterpreting concepts is reduced, by the use of technology structure of learning process becomes more effective, it makes teaching more realistic.

Technology is linked with major areas of student centred learning, we have all seen the advantages of technology use in present system of education and if quality can be maintained in education system then use of technology is a significant tool and facilitator.

## References

Adams, D. and Hamm, M. (1996). *Cooperative Learning—Critical Thinking and Collaboration Across the CURRICULUM*. Springfield, IL: Charles C. Thomas.

Bonwell, C.C. and Eison, J.A. (1991). *Active Learning: Creating Excitement in the Washington,* George Washington University: School of Education and Human Development.

Good, C.V. (1973). *Dictionary of Education*. New York: McGraw Hill.

McCombs, B.L. (1991). Motivation and Lifelong Learning. *Educational Psychologist*. 26(2): 117-127.

Slavin, R.E. (1997). *Educational Psychology: Theory and Practice*. Boston: Allyn & Bacon.

Stiggins, R.J. (1997). *Student-centred Classroom Assessment* (2nd ed.). Columbus, OH: Merrill Prentice-Hall.

http://www.intime.uni.edu

www.coreknowledge.org

# 6

# Use of Technology in School Education

## A Study of Selected Schools in Ajmer

*Zainab Farhat* and *Nagendra Ambedkar Sole*

> *"The Government of India would like to bring out a National Education Policy to see the changing dynamics of the population's requirement with regards to quality education, innovation and research, aiming to make India a knowledge superpower by its students with the necessary skills and knowledge and to eliminate the of manpower in science, technology, academics and industry."*
>
> ***—Ministry of Human Resource Development (MHRD), Government of India***

> *"There can be infinite uses of the computer and of new age technology, but if teachers themselves are not able to bring it into the classroom and make it work, then it fails."*
>
> ***—Nancy Kassebaum***

Technology acts as a tool to change the nature of learning. The future is about access, learning and collaboration, both locally and globally. Technology is now being developed as a key issue in the quality of learning process. The interest in quality arises from the need to combat the increasing competitiveness to have quality in education and from the need to have a global brand name among the leading educational institutions. Further to combat the issue of quality management, the issue of modernization of education cannot be overlooked. The demand for modernizing further accelerates high quality teaching which cannot be met without high quality teacher training. There is a need for teacher's education institutions to make ways for continuously improving the academic staff, design and delivery of curriculum, administrative procedures and support services in the most possible new form. It is well known fact that effective teachers can accelerate student learning, but too little is known about what makes a teacher effective.

The drive for an inclusive education is visible across all sectors in India and education has also come up into its ambit where introduction of the Aakash tablet was designed to improve the teaching process. The curriculum and theory have changed from the olden days, though India has no such strategy for technology in the classroom, but entrepreneurs and non-profits are braving the odds in the sector, they are coming up with new projects and plans to enhance the involvement of Information and Communication Technology in combating with the increasing importance of Technology in Education and Employment.

In two prominent speeches over the past month, Prime Minister Shri Narendra Modi has emphasised his aspiration to digitalise the education, seeing technology as a means to improvise the access to quality learning. This is in continuation with his government's previous announcements about making schools E-enabled, rolling out broadband highways, preparing children for a knowledge society, budget allocations towards virtual classrooms and on-line courses. While digitalizing education is clearly a goal to be met, the challenge is determining how this will be realized as after fully understanding the scope of technology in transforming the Education sector.

The call of today's educational environment is innovation and part of that environment is encompassed by having talent with the right skills and public policy that allows innovation to occur through fundamentals related to the infrastructure, and the whole area of information and communication technologies. A lot of it is public policy related to quality of education and the education curriculum. The other part of public policy relates to ease of doing business for the development of innovation to really grow.

## History of Education in India

The education system which we are in touch today has a very long journey, started in ancient period involving the *Gurukul, Parishad* and *Sammelans* considered as the agencies of education. Takshashila was the first university established in 700 BC and Nalanda was considered the biggest centre of education in the entire South Asia.

The trace of education system in British period was totally different and was determined by the needs of the colonial power. Education policy of British India was guided by the practical administrative needs of the colonialist. The British rulers did not take the adequate measures to help in the development of science and technology in India. Problems of educational reconstruction were reviewed by several commissions and committees, notably the University Education Commission (1948-49) and the Secondary Education Commission (1952-53). Some steps to implement the recommendations of these Commissions were taken; and with the passing of the Resolution on Scientific Policy under the leadership of Pandit Jawaharlal Nehru, the development of science, technology and scientific research received special emphasis in the country. The National Policy on Education, 1968 has suggested about the continuous effort to expand educational opportunity; a sustained and intensive effort to raise the quality of education at all stages; an emphasis on the development of science and technology (MHRD, 1968).

The development of the nation that was traditionally-bound society depended on a pervasive social transformation of the people which could be brought through the most powerful instrument, i.e. education. This was the vision of Kothari Education Commission (KEC) which was appointed to prepare a blueprint of a national pattern of education. KEC firmly believed, and made its recommendations, that it is the development of human resources, involving changes in the knowledge, skills, interests and values of the people as a whole, that will solve India's long pending problems. The Commission thus stressed that this direct link between education, human resource development, and national development exists only when the national system of education is properly organized, both qualitatively and quantitatively and it is reflected in the quality and number of persons coming out of our schools and colleges (Siddiqui, 2012).

The National Policy on Education 1986 emphasized on 'Operation Blackboard' (OB). The purpose of OB was to ensure provision of minimum essential facilities in primary schools—material facilities as well as learning equipment. Use of the word

'Operation' implies that there is urgency in this programme that goals are clear and well defined, and that government and the people are determined to achieve those goals within a predetermined timeframe (MHRD, National Policy on Education, 1986).

Sam Pitroda, Chairman, National Knowledge Commission which is a think tank in charge with making policies on knowledge and intensive service sector says, that the education system has to be changed from spoon-feeding to instilling inquisitiveness in students and encouraging them. He also added that education is not just constructing buildings; it is about content, quality and people. So our limitation at this point may not be just money. We need to focus on new processes and innovation.

Recognising the fundamental role of education in nurturing and fostering an ecosystem of innovation, the National Innovation Council is engaged in a series of initiatives to encourage innovation in existing educational institutions—universities, colleges and schools, as well as promoting new educational models and innovative platform for Knowledge creation, dissemination and application (GoI, 2010).

According to the World Bank, in 2010-14, only 15 per cent Indians had access to internet. Under the ICT, school scheme, the Government has spent a total of Rs. 2,585 crore since 2004 to install infrastructure in schools. Yet, by 2013-14, only 60 per cent secondary schools were equipped with computers. Programmes such as this have failed, often due to the lack of a comprehensive vision that links the use of technology for improving student learning, building teacher capacity or providing better governance (Dhawan, 2015).

## ICT Infrastructure: How Well Equipped are Our Schools?

The Growing version of Information and Communication Technology (ICT) has brought in rapid changes. It has made its entry in the school education system because of its appropriateness and applicability in the use of classroom teaching. It is well-known fact that the ICT has great potential for improving the teaching-learning process as it facilitates individualized learning and develops problem-solving skills. Educationists and teachers believe that with the help of ICT, the quality of education provided to the students can be significantly improved.

The transformation of educational technology is more important in Indian context because we are having a massive deficit of access to high quality education at the primary and high school level due to a number of challenges, ranging from geographical distribution to socio-economic condition of the learners who attend the Indian schools. Even the cost of educating one of the world's greatest populations has been gradually increasing, and there is an expectation that technology can make education affordable for those who are so far unable to benefit from the same.

In the era of digital communication, both students and teachers have an easy access to sources of information. But, to make use of it, firstly, the teachers need to be competent enough about the various information technologies and their potential uses. It is relevant to expose the teachers to information technology to realize its benefits for them and for the students. Secondly, teachers should update their knowledge and skills in using ICT as with the changing teaching methods in curriculum transaction, it is essential for teachers to adopt new technologies.

To analyse the usefulness and the extent of usage of technology in schools a study was conducted in 3 schools of Ajmer district of Rajasthan which were—

1. Rajkiya Madhyamika Vidyalaya, Badbao—a Government school.
2. Khwaja Model School—an affordable private school.
3. Sophia Senior Secondary School—a Christian Minority Institution.

The study is a purely qualitative analysis, looking into the conditions of the schools through the lenses of technological advancement they acknowledge till now. The technique used to collect data was observational study and group discussion method with the teachers and the students.

## Indicators for Technology Check: Glimpses from the Schools

### *1. The Extent of its Availability*

If children are needed to excel in the fast-changing, global society, so schools must harness the technological resources they need to function in a digital age. The accessibility and availability in terms of quality education through technology is the first priority to be taken up, as we must remember the commitment to future when we set priorities and justify the established policies. Government schools serve the majority of children in our country as these schools have witnessed a decline in their services, though increasingly they are accessed by the poor and the marginalised.

- The availability of technology in the Government school visited was next to none. It was the same like any other Government school, going in the same system since years. They did not have a proper computer lab, leave about smart classrooms. In barely 5 classrooms children from 1 to 10th class were accommodated and the computer lab consisted of 7 computers with dirt on it showing their non-usage from months. Other than the computer lab, no use of technology was seen in the school, the traditional teaching was more used with the black-board and chalk fulfilling every responsibility of making digital India.
- Affordable private schools (APS) are a fast growing chain of private schools in the developing world creating an educational alternative to government schools for low-income families. Parents these days choose APS in the perception that private schools provide higher quality education than government schools, and because APS are primarily English-medium schools. They are an alternative of government funded and High class school. The APS visited was not an ideal case or much better than the Government, but what it had was a better working computer lab and white boards in 5 classes. The computer lab was used only in the computer classes and the senior secondary was exposed to ppt classes for some lessons in the computer lab itself, there was neither any projector in classes nor smart classrooms, on enquiring with the officials they told that the demo smart classes were undertaken, but the real application still needs to be taken place.
- The third school is a Missionary English medium school

with a lot of technological innovations. There is a computer lab with 40 computers, smart classrooms, well equipped labs and projectors. The school focuses on high usage of technology. The school sister focuses on teacher's training to keep themselves abreast of emerging issues, share knowledge, and reach out to students. Several portals are being developed where teachers can network and share information including best practices.

### 2. *Teacher's Competency*

Teaching is a complex activity and Teacher's training is the most important aspect involving technological proficiency too. The quality of teacher defines the quality of education provided.

- The Government school had missed the teacher to teach computer, the classes were either wasted or some other teacher took over to teach them with their little knowledge. Earlier a computer teacher uses to come to take regular classes, but after the scheme got over there was no professional teacher even to take care of the computer labs as told by authority. As discussed with the teachers, they were enthusiastic to be a part of any technological innovation if started by the government as they too wished to make the classes more interesting. It was the lack of any government schemes for technological advancement that hindered the process of making government schools techno-friendly. Even the teachers when enquired were in favour of training classes for them as the curriculum was very monotonous and going on from years. Thus, they had zeal to learn to produce innovation if given a chance.
- The Khwaja Model School had 2 computer teachers taking the classes for the students starting from class 1. Rest most of the teachers were competent enough to make use of excel sheet and ppt for the exam and class purposes. Though the teachers never use any technology in the classroom or any other teaching aid, it was purely traditional method of teaching-learning. They had lack of time to experiment with any new method, thus adhered to the old methods. One teacher of secondary section

Meenakshi told that when she joined the school, she started using some models and presentation for teaching the students, e.g. showing the Human Digestive System, but the students were not interested to learn as they know that this method of teaching is long and time taking, they wanted the class to finish early.

- The Missionary school visited had teachers who have access to infrastructure and were given the opportunity to develop the expertise to use the machines and software tools. In that way they were competent enough to make use of every technology they were upkeeping with. In the primary section classes were taken through white boards and smart classrooms were used from time-to-time. In the secondary section there was wide use of computers and projectors to make the students learn about new development. The teachers were strictly told to make use of projectors after every class. A teacher of class 4th Stella told that the students wait for the projector to get started. They are full of inquisitiveness that what will be taught to them today.

### 3. *Student's Interest*

Ensuring quality Education and building-up the interest of the students is necessary for transforming society. As it is being increasingly spoken that even after spending large sums of money on programmes and schemes, countries have not become fully literate, so, it is time that more innovative and cost effective methods be put in place to address the problem of education.

- If the interest of the students is being mapped, the education system can work wonders for their change in life. The condition of the government school in India is crumbling down day-by-day as they are being forced to study the age old material with no newness. The children in the school are never taught through new skills, and it was a disheartening condition to see the future of the country sitting on the floors of the classroom. Only the 9th and 10th class were taken to the computer room that too rarely. The junior class had never been taken to any such lab and they complained that they were not being taught even leave about the newness in teaching.

- A new feature came into scene that the students of the APS, Khwaja Model, were not much familiar to study through techniques, though everyone of them was aware of about new applications and systems in the mobile phones. In fact one student of 12th class helped the web administrator to make the school website. Rest they were so much exposed to the traditional teaching that they only took computers as another period of teaching and never imbibed that into their curriculum.
- The girls of Sophia School were smart enough to talk about every technology they were using. Even the students of 4th and 5th classes knew about the availability and importance of technology in life. They had a CD with many of their subject book which they used at home to know more about the subjects. They even had science fest and maths fest in which they prepared the models and senior classes made projects and presentations. In that way the authorities of that school has a clear vision that effective use of ICTs can contribute to the timely transmission of information and knowledge, further helping education systems to meet this challenge.

### *4. Administrative Management*

Although there is a great opportunity for improvement in school education through the use of ICTs but the road to achieve that it is not easy. It will take on continued commitment from all stakeholders involved and the main amongst is the administrative staff which can make substantial and sustainable change. The prime work of Administration in school is to make policies and programmes.

- The Government school had no such effective administrative staff that plans for undertaking new programmes, though the State Education Board is responsible for channelizing the policies, in spite of having computers, they never took interest to make it reachable to the students.

- The APS though had many plans to formulate new schemes, but they were still under process. They had a vision of introducing smart classrooms and projector in every class in coming period. The administration was supporting enough as told by the teachers to listen to them about any new development they wish to keep.
- Sophia school had an effective administrative management as they keep in touch with the parents through SMS if the student remains absent. The administration works to get in touch with new technology. They have proper monitoring and evaluation system to keep a check on the student and teacher's working pattern.

## Challenges and Strategies in Introducing Technologies to Classroom

There are many challenges in implementing ICTs effectively in existing schools. The Policy-makers need to give ICTs adequate priority and attention so as to get in the benefits of deploying ICTs in school education especially Government schools.

We are living in a world where text messages, photos and files are transmitted within seconds to others. Latest mobiles and iphones have allowed us to connect to the internet through wireless networks and have revolutionized the way we share information and communicate with each other. Thus, rapid evolution of these modern information and communication technologies (ICTs) has also changed the language of pedagogy and learning. The introduction of ICT teaching has opened new horizons for teachers to have more interactive and learner-centred classroom environment.

Every educator wants students to learn to maximum extent. We cannot just tell educators that they need to use boxes and wires in the schools simply because they are expensive or because students need to know how to use the latest gadget. There has to be a reason of how technological tools will help them achieve the goals not met through the traditional method of tools.

- ***Providing Access to Technology***—Technology cannot become a meaningful support to students' work if they have limited access to it. Schools are often faces the problem of a limited budget for equipment and software (and even more limited inventory of the most powerful equipment) and make hard choices about how to get the most out of what they have. Technology is an exploration. But, before it can be used effectively, exploration must be valued as important to both teaching and learning. The Government School and the APS (Khwaja Model School) both lacked a wide access to these. The government school was not even in its infancy to start, though the Khwaja Model School started with some of it but not completely.

- ***Availability of Funds to Implement ICTs***—The crisis of budgetary and resource constraints of various governments, a widespread investment in ICTs in education is not easily possible. It was the lack of realization of the importance of technology that has not made investment in the government schools and the APS. Though Sophia School too need more innovations in terms of access of material resources other than the curriculum to compete at the national level. Yet, it had sufficient funds to channelize. It is important to understand the cost-benefit use of the wide range of ICT options in order to effectively target and spend the scarce resources. It is not possible to successfully implement the technology because of the high cost associated with acquiring, maintaining, and maximizing the use of ed-tech tools.
- ***Capacity Building of Teachers***—In the schools, the teachers are overloaded, less motivated and inadequately trained, and often deal with inconvenient working conditions. The government school teachers are not exposed to appropriate form of teacher training. They do not know how to make use of computers other than just taking the basic level learning class. Even the APS was an English medium school, but it lacked any new innovative training for the teachers, they were over occupied with their own traditional way of teaching. It is to be known that the use of ICTs in the classroom does not reduce the role of the teacher; neither does it automatically change teaching practices. In such a tone, building the capacity of teachers is required so that they are well equipped to deal with using ICTs in classrooms is a challenge.

- ***Lack of monitoring, evaluation and awareness***—Many of the issues and challenges associated with ICTs in education initiatives are known only by policy-makers and educators. There is a lack of good monitoring and evaluation tools and processes which can monitor things timely and where evaluation data is available of much of the work. The things visibly noticed after visiting the first two schools was that nobody is interested to take the move ahead of changing the situation. As resistance is commonly witnessed while attempting to introduce ICTs in most of the schools, very often from the teachers, since they will become over burdened once technology comes in or due to the perception that it is too late for them to adapt to a new environment. There is also a general lack of awareness about the utility of ICTs in education and how they can be accessed and utilized economically and effectively. This lack of awareness and knowledge about ICTs and their use in education, even on the part of policy-makers, administrators and educators, makes it particularly difficult to deploy ICTs in the field of school education.
- ***Knowledge Gaps***—A common reason that technology is not effectively implemented is because the school's intentions are not matched by knowledge of technology's potential. Many school leaders and teachers are still unaware of how to make use of technology in its full capacity and till what extent.

## What Needs to be Done?

Those days are over when we just tell students who Albert Einstein was, it is time to show them who he actually was and what works he did through a whole video or images and it can evaluate learning in multiple ways, instead of relying only on traditional paper and pencil tests. Books can only accommodate a certain amount of information, technology is a world in itself, you just browse a single term, and the whole theory of that term appears through internet. The knowledge in books are things what happened in the past that too in a limited way but through internet and communication technology it can be shown of what happening in that subject currently. It is essential to revolutionize ourselves, our students, our administrators, and policy-makers throughout the country tc make the best use of the technology tools available.

- The government can establish autonomous agencies in every state, similar to that of the National Skill Development Corporation, to encourage innovation and develop the environment for digital learning solutions. The autonomous agency can further be staffed with talent from the private sector and fund and private operators to create these platforms.
- School leaders should find solutions that have curriculum aligned with the technological change. For smaller classes the content should be according to their age group and little amount of introduction to computers so that from their roots itself children become well accustomed to newness. The schools should be prepared to align to the new standards being established. The content should be designed for the lower classes in an attractive manner as it is an important developmental age. Solutions should be build that do not require immense planning on the teachers' part.
- Access to technology is only one piece of the puzzle. We need to solve the concept of E-enabled schools, and formulate clear goals and objectives for the introduction of ICT in education. Most policy documents have viewed technology either as a substitute for teachers when the traditional education system is unavailable, or as the narrow lens of "technical skills for a knowledge society". But, if technology is to be made as mainstream, its objectives must go beyond this, and should be directed to a more profound change in the system.
- Digital India is an opportunity to push ourselves ahead in the use of technology. The system should not duplicate the mistakes of the past by assuming that providing hardware and connectivity to schools will result in the adoption of technology. Instead, a vision should be approached and commitment should be made to

approach to usage of technology to improve the education system.

- Despite the challenges outlined, ICTs are being increasingly used in education in both developed and developing world, in order to reach out to children for providing them with quality education, and to equip them with a wider range of educational resources. Thus, a common pattern of curriculum needs to be made to introduce technology in education.
- Finally, teachers must educate themselves on how to make the best use of tools to enhance teaching and learning. As education technology is a growing area, it should be track closely to understand its effectiveness. Lastly, measures should be made to facilitate the scaling up of innovations that have impact on student learning.

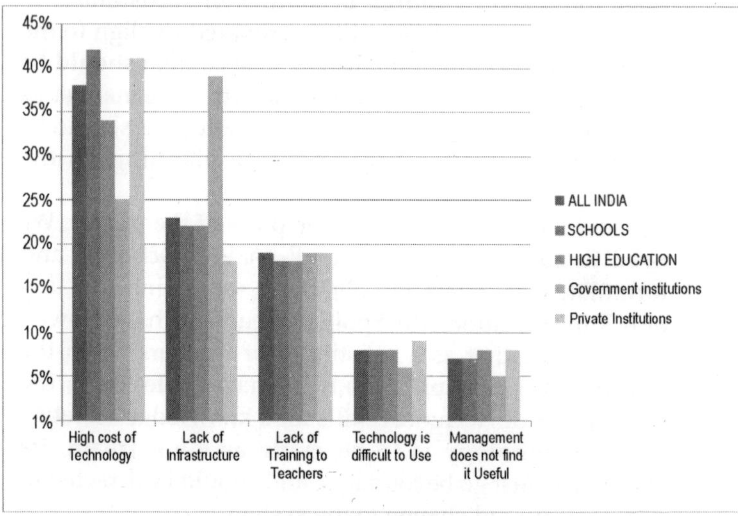


*Source:* Pearson Voice of Teacher Survey 2015.

**Fig 6.1:** Challenges in Technology Adoption

## Glimpses from the Schools Visited

- The visit in the 3 schools of Ajmer district of Rajasthan was carried out from 19th-24th October, 2015.

**Fig. 6.2:** Use of Projector in Classroom

**Fig. 6.3:** Picture of the Classroom

**Fig. 6.4:** A Well Maintained Computer Laboratory

## References

Dhawan, N.D. (2015, July 8). *The Digital India Push for Education*. Retrieved October 2015, from *The Financial Express*. www.financialexpress.com.

*Education Technology in India: Designing Ed-tech* for affordable Private Schools.

GoI (2010). National Innovation Council. Retrieved from http://innovationcouncilarchive.nic.in

MHRD (1968). http://www.teindia.nic.in

MHRD (1986). National Policy on Education.

Pearson Voice of Teacher Survey—Helping Shape India's New Education Policy, 2015.

Rajasekar, S. and Vaiyapuri, Raja, P. (2007). Higher Secondary School Teachers' Computer Knowledge and Their Attitude towards Computer. *Journal of All India Association for Educational Research*, 19, (1): 70-76.

Sadik, A. (2006) Factors Influencing Teachers' Attitudes toward Personal use and school Use of Computers New Evidence From A Developing Nation, *Evaluation Review*, 30(1) 86-113.

Siddiqui, M.A. (2012). *Education in India*.

Uniyal, N.P. and Pandey, S.K. (2008). Teachers' attitude towards computer in relation to sex, age, locality and experience. *Experiments in Education*, 36, (1).

Wood, T.L., Putney, D., and Cass, M.A. (1997). Accessibility: The Main Factor Influencing Special Education Teachers' Perceived Level of Computer Competence. *Journal of Computing in Teacher Education*, 13(4): 20-24.

Zhao, Y. (2007). Social studies teachers' perspectives of technology integration. *Journal of Technology and Teacher Education*, 15 (3): 311-333.

# 7

# Need of Introducing Technology Based Education in Rural India

*Shobhani Saxena*

## Introduction

Villages are the backbones of India. These villages are mostly dependent on agriculture. In villages, less importance is given to education. To increase the villagers' interest in education, government has facilitated the rural schools by providing many facilities like free food (mid-day meal), free books, scholarships and other incentives. Government is also facilitating towards creating/improving a quality education environment. The development of a country primarily depends on its education system. Literacy is another proper indicator of economic development. India is still a developing nation since its education system lacks behind as compared to other developed nations, it is important that we must understand the need of education and its role in carving future of Indian youth. There are many areas which are to be studied regarding development of education system in India. Information technology can play a very vital role in developing the rural education system. It ensures awareness among the rural population about importance of education. Indian education system has got contribution from both public as well as private sector; it is controlled by Central Government as well as State Governments.

## Overview of Indian Education System

Education is the most important lever for social, economic and political transformation. A well-educated population, equipped with the relevant knowledge, attitudes and skills is essential for economic and social development of country in the twenty-first century. In order to achieve Universalization of Elementary Education (UEE), the Government of India has initiated a number of programmes and projects. The Government adopts an integrated approach in the implementation of the various centrally sponsored schemes, in keeping with principles of the national policy on education, to ensure that the education of equitable quality for all to fully harness the nation's human resource potential. The common objectives are to enhance access through the expansion of quality school education; to promote equity through the inclusion of disadvantaged groups and weaker sections, and to improve the quality of education. Following is the list of centrally sponsored programmes being implemented in the Education Sector under Ministry of Human Resource Development (*See* Table 7.1).

## Challenges Faced by Students in Rural Areas

There exist a number of barriers faced by village students; however, some of the common barriers can easily be solved by providing proper education. It would be much more relevant and easier to bring improvements—

### *Faculty*

Adequate teachers are not present to deliver education; the main reason behind this is low wages. Since, low salary is paid to the village school teachers, people are not willing to teach in rural schools and this leads to poor quality education and teachers pay less attention to the students. Many times a single teacher teaches all the offered subjects to a particular class.

### *Infrastructure*

Village schools usually do not have proper infrastructure especially

**Table 7.1:** Programmes Sponsored by Central Government (HRD)

| *Sl. No.* | *Name of the Scheme* |
|---|---|
| 1. | Sarva Shiksha Abhiyan (SSA) |
| 2. | Kasturba Gandhi Balika Vidyalaya |
| 3. | National Programme for Education of Girls at Elementary Level (NPEGEL) |
| 4. | Mid-Day Meal Scheme (MDMS) |
| 5. | Mahila Samakhya |
| 6. | Rashtriya Madhyamik Shiksha Abhiyan (RMSA) |
| 7. | Scheme for setting-up of 6000 Model Schools at Block level as Benchmark of Excellence |
| 8. | Scheme for Construction and Running of Girl's Hostel for Secondary and Higher Secondary Schools |
| 9. | Scheme of Vocationalization of Secondary Education at +2 level |
| 10. | Scheme of ICT School |
| 11. | Inclusive Education for the Disabled at Secondary School (IEDSS) |
| 12. | Quality Improvement in School |
| 13. | Strengthening of Teachers' Training Institutions |
| 14. | Adult Education and Skill Development Scheme |
| 15. | Scheme for providing a Quality Education in Madarsas (SPQEM) |
| 16. | National Means-*cum*-Merit Scholarship Scheme |
| 17. | Scheme for Infrastructure Development in Minority Institutions (IDMI) |
| 18. | National Scheme for Incentive to the Girl Child for Secondary Education |
| 19. | Appointment of Language Teachers |
| 20. | Setting-up of New Polytechnics and Strengthening of Existing Polytechnics |
| 21. | Pre-metric Scholarship Scheme |
| 22. | Eklavya Model Residential School (EMRS) |

schools managed by government sector. Adequate classrooms are not available and most of the time the students belonging to lower classes study in open grounds or beneath some old big tree. Sometimes students of different classes have to share a single class. Also absence of toilets is a big issue. Girls and boys need to share a single toilet which is used even by the teaching staff in some cases.

### *Lack of Transport Facilities and Study Material*

Extremely backward villages do not have their own schools and hence parents need to send their children in nearby villages or cities for getting education but due to lack of transport facilities, children cannot travel far to come to school. Apart from this children do not have proper textbooks according to their current syllabus.

**Rural School Education System**

In India, condition of some of the rural school is still not good, financially they are week. There are schools in rural areas where students have to walk/travel far away distances to avail school facilities. Most of the rural schools do not have proper infrastructure. Rural students need better direction and guidance in learning. They do not have direction to choose the study materials. Rural students are quite enthusiastic and hard working in nature. If efforts are made in right direction, then drastic development is possible. For betterment we expect that every rural education system should have the following:

(i) Sufficient number of schools.
(ii) Good transportation facilities to avoid children walking miles to reach the schools.
(iii) Basic amenities like drinking water.
(iv) Advanced education.
(v) Computer education and computer training.
(vi) Group classes should be taken by using video-conferencing and audio-conferencing.
(vii) The teachers should get facilities with tools like laptops, printers to provide notes and other important notices to the children.
(viii) Better infrastructure, as sometimes children are even made to sit on the floor due to non-availability of furniture.
(ix) Computer aided teaching.
(x) Involving rural children in other learning activities like analytical, problem-solving, decision-making, sports, co-curricular activities and competitions.

Such events and activities tend to help in the overall development of the children. Some other identified needs for improving the rural education systems are:

(i) Quality education and adequate study materials.
(ii) Expert guidance in learning.
(iii) Sharing the knowledge about recent trends and opportunities.
(iv) Exposure of modern world.
(v) Proper guidance towards pursuing job-oriented courses.

## ICT for Improving Quality of Education

Today ICT has been become a revolution in all walks of life particularly in education. The ICT revolution has changed the learning process of childhood up to the real world. By E-learning today's children are enabled to develop a self-concept; develop basic decision-making skills. Today students require higher level of education to succeed in the new, knowledge-based society. E-learning most often means an approach to facilitate and enhance learning by means of personal computers, CD-ROMs, audio-visual aids and the Internet. This includes e-mail, discussion forums, and collaborative software. ICT offers new opportunities to strengthen many aspects of early childhood education practice such as—

- An opportunity to support and enhance children's learning and plays experiences;
- Opportunities to support and strengthen practitioners' professional learning and development; and
- Opportunities to support and strengthen relationships and communication between early childhood centres, parents, and other people connected to the early childhood education setting.

## Advanced Technology and Tools

School in rural areas are still far behind in using technologies such as e-learning, the only way of teaching there is using a blackboard and chalk, but in many places modern path of using communication technologies is adopted like televisions and radios. In India (2004), EDUSAT was launched to support education, ISRO launched EDUSAT successfully for presenting the education videos; currently, due to advancement in internet technologies with respect to speed and high coverage advanced internet technologies and tools like Virtualization, Cloud technologies and MOODLE can also be used.

### *1. Cloud Computing*

Cloud computing not being a hardware technology offers various ways for educational purpose. Cloud computing allows organizations to increase computing capacity or add computing capabilities without need to invest in infrastructure or train additional personnel. It acts as an off-site, on-line server and offers a robust and flexible way to store important data or programmes and to save money without requiring additional service personnel or physical storage technology. This system was piloted in 2008 for 192 schools around the capital city and the Ministry of Education is considering expanding the service to reach an additional 350 schools.

### 2. *MOODLE*

Modular Object-Oriented Dynamic Learning Environment (MOODLE) is a on-line learning service for courses that are internet based, it also provides educational websites. It has features such as: Assignment submission, Discussion forum, Files download, Grading, MOODLE instant messages, on-line calendar, on-line news and announcement, on-line quiz. It has many tools to enhance students and teachers experience in a course, such as: Assignments, Chats, Choices, Databases Forums, Glossaries Lessons, Quizzes Resources, SCORM Surveys etc.

### 3. *Wikis*

Wikis provide vast information and it can be edited by anyone thus providing opportunity to everyone for placing their knowledge which can then be available to any person using it. Wikis are generally open sources and hence a cheaper way, Wikis' writing is easy to learn and incorporate with technical support available on-line. It can control to restrict unauthorized users. Wikis can be accessed from any browser and anywhere we want. It is a great teaching tool provided, it must be used wisely.

### 4. *On-line Media*

On-line Media also provides a way to implement modern ways to teach, students learn better by observation and visual presentation than hearing only; short videos which are available on-line help to understand things more clearly. For example: The working of technical instruments and tools could be understood more easily through videos rather than written text depicting their working.

## Creating an On-line Learning Environment

The obvious advantages to on-line training have tempted many instructors to jump too soon to exploit web-based teaching (WBT). To create an effective on-line learning environment, it is important to pause and consider a few practical and pedagogical issues, including the on-line roles of instructor and student, the best type of technology tools to use, and the process of collaboration. It is also important to consider how materials will be distributed, how students will be assessed, and how specialized software will be incorporated into the learning environment.

### *1. Roles*

The instructor must accept the role of facilitator (as opposed to leader) in the learning process. This change requires moving from the "chalk-and-talk" role to a "guide-on-the-side" role. It is also important that instructors realize that self-directed learning requires high motivation on the part of the students.

### *2. Technology*

Students must have access to a standard Web browser and Internet connection. Instructors must of course be familiar with HTML tools and the process of converting a traditional course for use on the Web.

### *3. Collaboration Tools*

Effective collaboration between the instructor and students is crucial. Instructors must be familiar with the many internet technologies that support effective communication and collaboration, including e-mail, group discussion lists, text-based chat facilities, and even desktop video-conferencing.

### *4. Material Distribution*

The Web provides a platform for delivering not only the text materials that a class might need, but the multimedia requirements as well, including audio and video streams of instructor lectures.

Instructors must be familiar with the strengths and weaknesses of current technologies even if other people will be converting classroom lectures into digital video for the web because understanding what the web is capable of doing will help determine the website's content.

### 5. Student Assessment

Computer-based testing, sometimes called computer-managed instruction (CMI) can provide instant feedback on student comprehension of course materials. But this type of managed testing cannot work unless instructors accept assignments and provide feedback to students electronically.

### 6. Implications of New Technologies

**Table 7.2:** Implications of New Technologies

| *Traditional Model of Teaching* | *New Model of Teaching* | *Technology Implications* |
|---|---|---|
| Classroom Lectures | Individual Exploration | Availability of networked computers with guided access to on-line information and learning materials |
| Teacher as Deliverer of Information | Teacher as a Guide | Teaching *via* programme websites and on-line learning environments; access to external experts over the internet |
| Individual Work | Collaborative Learning | Access to e-mail and on-line 'conferencing' tools |
| Face-to-face Teaching | Flexible and Distance Learning | Student access to networked computers for materials delivery and support |
| Consistent Content | Fast-changing Content | Availability of networks, web space and web publishing tools; sharing of computer-based learning materials with other institutions |

## Conclusion

Information and communication technology has great relevance in today's world. If implemented properly ICT can surely bridge the gap between economically and technology backward students and rest of them. With the IT boom in India technology is easily accessible to the government machineries with relevantly cheaper and convenient manner. Proper training and implementation of ICT programmes in simple way and language which is easily understandable by the rural people can surely bring about revolution in rural development. We had enlightened educational conditions and environment of rural India. Use of Internet for education has a potential to change many aspects of our lives. Thus, WBE is Platform which is independent, convenient in access, cost saving, availability of easily updated contents and with emerging technologies it can be made more effective. Web-Based Learning adds human support through on-line tutor, extending the scope of what can be effectively taught into many new subject areas.

## References

Dinesha, H.A., Dr. V.K. Agrawal, (2011), Advanced Technologies and Tools for Indian Rural School Education System, *International Journal of Computer Applications* (0975-8887) Volume 36, No. 10, December.

Government of India. Ministry of Human Resource Development, Department of School Education and Literacy Department of Higher Education, *Annual Report, 2011-12,* pp. 22 and 186.

Stiemen, J. Managing Director, IICD. (November 2007). *ICT for Development and Education,* pp. 16-21, [On-line]. Available at www.iicd.org

*Status of Education in India,* www.infodev.org

Michael, W., *Rural Education,* Available at www.iitk.ac.in

# 8
# Tele-immersion in Education

*Nalini Misra*

Tele-immersion was originally defined in 1996 by Tom Defanti of Electronics Visualization laboratory, as *the union of networked virtual reality (VR) and video in the context of significant computing and data mining*. In the words of Jason Leigh, "The term Tele-immersion was first used as the title of a workshop to bring together researchers in distributed computing collaboration virtual reality and networking." It is a broad multi-disciplinary research area that includes all aspects of computer science, virtual worlds, Tele-operation and Tele-presence. A variety of network elements are required to scale up virtual environments to arbitrary sizes, simultaneously connecting thousands of interacting players and all kinds of information objects.

Tele-immersion enables users at geographically distributed sites to collaborate in real time in a shared, simulated, hybrid environment as if they were in the same physical room. Tele-immersion involves the construction of a three dimensional (3D), realistic holographic environment where two or more physically separated users can communicate with each other in real time. Simply stated Tele-immersion is the intersection of virtual reality (VR) and video-conferencing. Tele-immersion is an engineering solution to this deficiency and is made possible by combining state-of-the-art multimedia technologies with high-speed data transfer. Tele-immersion is a technology to be implemented with high speed internet that will enable users in different geographic locations to come together in a simulated environment to interact. Users will feel like they are actually looking, talking, and meeting with each other face-to-face in the same place, even though they may be miles apart physically.

## Tele-immersion and Virtual Reality

Some of the experts believe that Tele-immersion and the virtual reality are same things, but that is not true, there are major differences between the two technologies. Virtual reality is an artificial environment created with the help of computer hardware and software and presented to the user in such a way that it appears and feels like a real environment. Collaborative virtual reality is the use of two or more virtual reality environments and high performance networking to support synchronous collaboration focused on the same virtual reality models. Tele-immersion is defined on the integration of audio- and video-conferencing with a collaborative virtual reality environment. While virtual reality allows you to move in a computer generated 3D environment, Tele-immersion can only create a 3D environment that you can see but not interact with.

## Tele-immersion and Video-Conferencing

Tele-immersion is more than just a sophisticated mode of video-conferencing. Whereas video-conferencing is limited to moving images displayed on a computer screen and sound emerging from speakers, Tele-immersion aims to introduce realism and allow people to communicate with "more than just words." Ultimately, Tele-immersion allows people move around and converse in a realistic three dimensional space, make direct eye contact with each other, and even manipulate virtual objects together. Existing video-conferencing applications lack this dimensionality and realism. Although the basic premise of Tele-immersion is essentially the same as video-conferencing, its applications span a much broader range of fields.

## Historical Background

It was way back in 1965 that the great pioneer of the field of computer graphics, Ivan Sutherland, proposed the concept of the 'ultimate display'. It described a graphics display that would allow the user to experience a completely computer rendered environment. In 1998, Abilene, a backbone research project, was launched and now serves as a base for Internet-2 research. Internet-2 needed an application that would challenge and stretch its networks' capabilities. The head of advanced network and services proposed Tele-immersion at the application that could drive internet-2 research forward. That is how the national Tele-immersion initiative is framed in May 2000. Researchers at the Universities of North Carolina (UNC), the Universities of Pennsylvania and advanced network and services reached a milestone in developing this technology. A user sitting in an office at UNC in Chapel Hill, NC, was able to see life like, 3D images of colleagues hundreds of miles away, one in Philadelphia and the other in New York. Today scientists are still developing this new communication technology. There are several groups working together on the National Tele-immersion Initiative (NTII) to make this wonderful technology available to the common men.

**Internet-2**

This will replace the current internet infrastructure. It is a consortium made-up of the US Government, industry and academia (180 universities) that has been formed for creating tomorrow's internet. This new network will have a higher bandwidth and speed that can be 1000 times faster than today's internet. This high bandwidth and high speed network is necessary to transfer the large amounts of data that Tele-immersion will produce.

**How Tele-immersion Works?**

At the core Tele-immersion is the successful creation of a real time holographic environment. The three steps to construct a holographic environment are:

- The computer recognizes the presence and movements of people and objects.
- The computer tracks those images.
- The computer projects those images on a stereo immersive surface.

The result is 3D, life-size, realistic hologram that maintains lighting and depth, thus accounting for viewer perception. Holographic environments are generated by advanced computers that work at computing speeds thousands of times faster than PCs we use everyday in our routine life. The 3D reconstruction for Tele-immersion is facilitated by projecting images on a stereo-immersive surface using IT. Two or more cameras take rapid sequential shots of the same object, continuously performing distance calculations and projecting those into the computer-simulated environment, to replicate real-time movement. By mixing cameras and the Internet telephony, video-conferencing allows real-time exchange of a vast amount of information effectively, without the need of the physical presence of every person in one central room. Following the flow of information, Tele-immersion depends on intense data processing at each end of a connection, mediated by high performance network.

## Tele-cubicle

The Tele-immersion technology uses a "Tele-cubicle" which is equipped with large screens, scanners, sensors and cameras by means of which users communicate. It consists of a stereo-immersive desk surface and two stereo-immersive wall surfaces. These three display surfaces join to form a corner desk unit. Walls appear as windows to other users' environment, while desks join together to form a virtual conference table in the centre. This allows realistic inclusion of Tele-immersion into the work environment as it consumes the average amount of desk space.

## Display Technologies

Stereo-immersive displays present a clear view of the scenes being transmitted. Hepatic sensors allow people to touch projections as if these were real. And, desktop supercomputers complete trillions of calculations needed to create a holographic environment. Another possibility to support these environments could be a network of computers that split the total power.

- ***From the sender:*** Parallel processors accept visual inputs from the cameras and reinterpret the scene as a 3-Dimensional computer model.

- ***To the receiver*:** Specific rendering of remote people and places are synthesized from the model as it is received to match the point of view of each eye of a user. The whole process repeats many times in a second to keep up with the user head motion.

**Generating the 3-Dimensional Images**

1. An array of cameras views people and their surroundings from different angle. Each camera generates an image from its point of view many times in a second.
2. Each set of the images taken at a given instant is sorted into subsets of overlapping trios of images.
3. From each trio of images, a "disparity map" is calculated, reflecting the degree of variation among the images at all points in the Disparity map visual-field. The disparities are then analyzed to yield depths that would account for the differences between what each camera sees. These depth values are combined into a "bas relief" depth map of the scene.
4. All the depth maps are combined into a single viewpoint independent sculptural model of the scene at a given moment. Process of combining the depth maps provide maps opportunities for removing spurious points and noise.

Tele-immersion requires supercomputers to perform the trillions of calculations that are needed to portray 3D environments. The ultimate goal of Tele-immersion is not to reproduce a real face-to-face meeting in every detail, but to provide the next generation interface for collaborators worldwide, to work together in a virtual environment (VE) that is seamlessly enhanced by computation and large databases. Tele-immersive environments will, therefore, facilitate not only interaction between users themselves, but also between users and computer generated models and simulations. This will require expanding the boundaries of computer vision, tracking, display, and rendering technologies. As a result, all of this will enable users to achieve a compelling experience and it will lay the groundwork for a higher degree of the inclusion into the entire system.

## Challenges of Tele-immersion

(1) Reliability of connection and transfer of speed between the computers and supercomputer.
(2) The computers also have a limited band width to handle very large data.
(3) The networks must be in place and tuned to support high-bandwidth applications.
(4) Multicast, unicast, reliable and unreliable data transmissions called "flows", need to be provided for and managed by the networks and the operating systems of supercomputer class workstations.
(5) Real time considerations for video- and audio-reconstruction "streaming" are critical for achieving the feel of Tele-presence, whether synchronous or recorded and played back.
(6) Quite enough computing and bits/second to fully analyze, and simulate reality for scientific purposes.
(7) Immersion wants everything: real time and best depths and construction of the 3D scene in a real time taking into account the best depths is a more challenging task.

## Advantages of Tele-immersion

When Tele-immersion technology will be easily be available to the world for research, education and business, it will completely change our life. No longer will people have to travel long distances at great expense in order to conduct business meetings. All that would be available with the click of mouse by using Tele-immersion system to set-up a virtual shared conference room with participants separated by thousands of miles of physical space, but being able to interact as if they were in the same room.

When Tele-immersion technology becomes cheap enough for personal use, the way we interact with the world will change as well. Instead of getting into a car and driving hundreds of miles or flying in a plane for thousands of miles, one can instantly visit his/her friends and relatives, seeing them and interacting with them will be experienced as if they were right in front of you. If you are working late and will not be present at home for dinner, you can still be home for dinner through Tele-immersion, having dinner with your spouse and children in a virtual dining room.

## Application of Tele-immersion in Education

The extensive nature of Tele-immersion makes it applicable for communication in almost any line of work or sphere of life. The primary intent of Tele-immersion is to promote global communication and interaction, and therefore, it can be incorporated in various fields such as medicine, engineering, architecture design, business conferencing, education, international relations, political affairs, travel, home entertainment, gaming, and much more.

In education, Tele-immersion can be used to bring together students sitting remote and rural areas in a single environment relationship among educational institutions could improve tremendously in the future with the use of Tele-immersion. This is particularly important when there is lack of specialist faculty at all required sites, and hence, the need to resort to distance education. This technology will result in a much higher level of collaboration among educational institutes. Already, the academic world is sharing information on research and development to better the end results. Tele-immersion can easily promote this collaboration. With Tele-immersion in schools, students could have access to data or control a telescope from a remote location, or meet the students from other countries by projecting themselves into a foreign space. Tele-immersion will bring to them place, equipment and situations earlier not available, helping them experience what they could have only watched, read or heard about earlier.

Tele-immersion will redefine long-distance education. Universities and schools will be able to transmit lectures over great distances, in real-time. Immersive electronic books will enrich students' learning experiences. Much like the Internet, Tele-immersion will be an immensely useful resource for scholars of all ages.

Tele-immersive environments will, therefore, facilitate not only interaction between users themselves, but also between users and computer generated models and simulations. This will require expanding the boundaries of computer vision, tracking, display, and rendering technologies. As a result, all of this will enable users to achieve a compelling experience and it will lay the groundwork for a higher degree of their inclusion into the entire system. This new paradigm for human computer interaction falls into the category of the most advanced network applications and, as such, it is the ultimate technical challenge for Internet.

## References

Ananthaswamy. (2000), *Tele-Immersion: Virtual Reality New Scientist.*
Bonsor, K. *How Holographic Environments will Work.*
Goldman, J. (2002) Computers Get Touchy-Feely, *TechLive.*
www.advanced.org
www.booksite.elsevier.com
www.cs.unc.edu
www.docs.google.com
www.howstuffw?orks.com

# 9

# Perception of Academicians towards Usage of Communication Technology

*Nidhi Singh* and *Rajeev Saxena*

## Introduction

In today's world usage of communication technology is increasing day-by-day. By the term communication technology, it is meant usage of internet through any means such as computer, laptop etc. as well as usage of smart phone. The KPMG report on Mobile India in January 2014 shows that there are 6.8 billion people on the planet and 4 billion out of them use mobile phones whereas only 3.5 billion use toothbrush. Figure 9.1 drawn by IAMAI shows how many internet users are there till June 2013.

While looking over the given data it could be estimated that how internet usage has grown yet the difference is there between urban and rural population. India is the third largest Smartphone market in the world. Fig. 9.2 shows how the usage of Smartphone is increasing at very fast pace in India.

Over 40 per cent of searches on Google originate from mobile phones. Mobile data traffic is ~9 per cent of total Internet Traffic. In Rural India, 70 per cent of the active internet users also access internet using mobile phones along with personal computer and laptop while 30 per cent consumers use internet only through mobile.

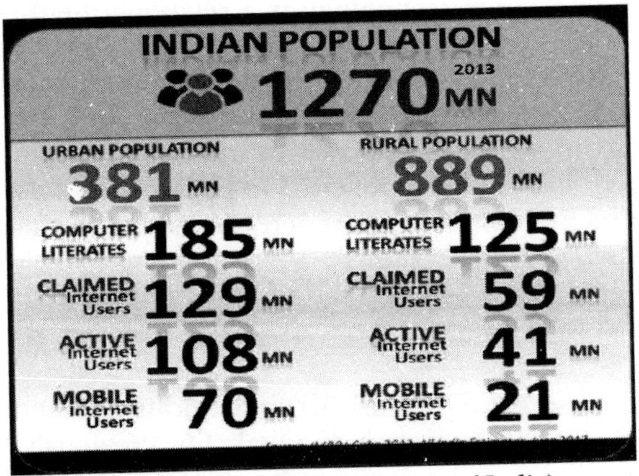


*Source:* IAMAI (Internet and Mobile Authority of India).

**Fig 9.1:** Indian Population

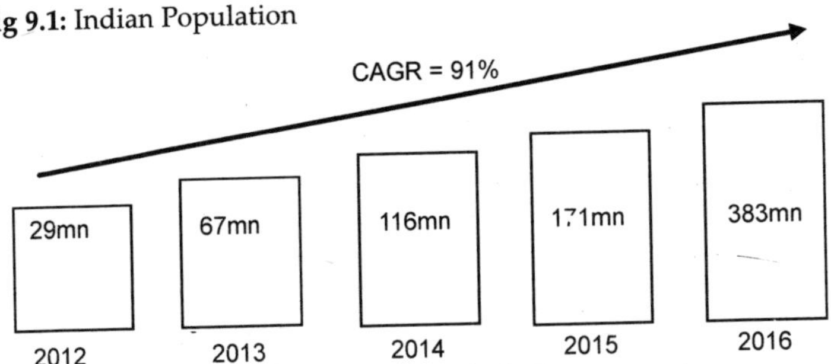


**Fig. 9.2:** Number of Smart Phone users in India
*Source:* IDC, Avendus estimates.

The term techno-stress was coined in 1984 by a clinical psychologist Brod (1984) sees Techno-stress as a modern disease of adaptation caused by an inability to cope with the new computer technologies in a healthy manner. It manifests itself in two distinct but related ways: in the struggle to accept computer technology, and in the more specialized form of over identification with computer technology. In my study techno-stress will be considered in the way as defined by Rosen and Weil (2000) 'techno-stress' as any negative impact on attitudes, thoughts, behaviours, or body physiology that is caused either directly or indirectly by technology. Techno-stress or psychosomatic illness caused by working with computer technology on a daily basis.

Communication technology is a relational field (simply, a medium that connects people) and its implications for human communication and listening. It tend to be one-way, taking people away from community activity and controlled by political economic interests—as opposed to interactive media channels which are, and have the potential to be, a means for extending interactive human communication (dependent on perception) Purdy (1997).

## Review of the Literature

In twenty-first century, the use of communication technologies has become a necessity in every individual's life. Previously, the usage of communication technologies such as internet was mostly limited to the organization (Ayyagari, 2012). But, with the advances, the interactions have decreased the boundaries of the usage for personal use or for work purpose. These kinds of usage force individuals to adjust their communication technology usage (Ayygari *et al.*, 2011). These adjustments range from integration of ICTs into workplace, to the fear of becoming obsolete, to the phenomenon of techno-stress. Many studies have been done on 'techno-stress' and the contributing factors.

Tarafdar *et al.*, 2011, state that emerging information systems (IS) for work are affecting professional users. Their study focused on data collected from information system users (N = 233) from two U.S. firms, and they thought of explaining why 'techno-stress' is created, how it differs among individuals and what are its adverse consequences. About 80 per cent of the respondents in this particular study felt that workplace information user has made their work more stressful through use of higher technology.

These authors stated that users experience techno-stress due to information overload, invasion of personal life, inability to deal with uncertainty and complexity of IS, and a sense of insecurity due to rapid advances in information system techno-stress may significantly reduce job satisfaction, commitment, innovation, and productivity. Users can quickly and easily access information, work from anywhere, and share information and insights with colleagues in real time. But these technologies can make them feel compulsive about being connected, forced to respond to work related information in real time, trapped in almost habitual multitasking and left with little time to spend on sustained thinking and creative analysis. These latter outcomes constitute the phenomenon of techno-stress.

These authors were the originators of the five techno-stress creating conditions. First is 'techno-overload' which describes situations where use of IS forces professionals to work more and work faster; trying to do more in less time, and experiencing tension and anxiety. Second is 'techno-invasion' which describes situations where professionals can potentially be reached anywhere and anytime and feel the need to be constantly connected. The regular workday extends into family hours including vacations. Due to this kind of continual connectivity, individuals feel attached to these technologies and experience intrusion on their time and space. Therefore, they experience frustration and stress. Third is the 'techno-complexity' which describes situations where the complexity associated with IS forces professionals to spend time and effort in learning and understanding how to use new applications. Users can find the variety of applications and functions intimidating and difficult to understand, and consequently feel stressed. The fourth is 'techno-insecurity' which emerges in situations where users feel threatened about losing their jobs to other people who have a better understanding of latest technology. It is common to find newer, often younger, recruits who come equipped with a higher comfort level in using modern technologies. Existing professionals may thus feel insecure or cynical about technology leading to tension and stress. Last is 'techno-uncertainty' which refers to contexts where continuing changes and upgrades to IS do not give professionals a chance to develop a base of experience for a particular application or system. They find this unsettling because their knowledge becomes rapidly obsolete. Although they may initially be enthusiastic about learning new applications and technologies, constant requirements for refreshing and updating eventually create frustration and anxiety. These findings were collected from structured interviews and surveys. Survey questions described potential stressful situations in the context of computer use. All items were measured on a five point Likert scale. Overall, the authors findings of the five techno-stress creating conditions are often referred to in other studies and have become the basis of techno-stress research.

According to Agbonlahor (2006), Universities all over the world are among the major organizations, where communication technologies resulted facilities are being used on a large scale to increase the productivity. However, while the benefits of adoption of communication technologies are high, it is also true that the adoption in teaching and learning habits and their daily usage of these communication technologies have brought about a number of demands and challenges such as techno-stress, productivity decrease and family problems. Usage of communication technologies (internet and Smartphones) leads to a number of issues some of which are further identified physical maladies such as "headaches, irritability, stomach or intestinal problems and heart related issues such as heart attack or high blood pressure". (Brillhart, 2004).

According to Odho and Odigbo (2013), "Techno-stress is result of altered habits of work and collaboration due to the use of modern information and communication technologies at workplace." A study was conducted by Jenal and Mahanti (2014) among academician in India and a result was drawn, which shows, three demographic factors, i.e., gender, age and technological awareness has a major influence on techno-stress. Results also concluded that there are significant influences of age, gender, technology awareness and tenure (duration of service) on techno-stress. But techno-stress has no impact on marital status of academician in India.

Some statement literally explains the exact meaning what technology usage are exactly doing (Weil, 1997), "Technology may do wonders for us, but it is also doing something to us." Information and Communication Technologies (ICTs) have merged into individuals' daily lives (Vodanovich, Sundaram, & Myers, 2010). ICT connectedness has been considered an emerging phenomenon that shows the importance of ICT in a person's everyday life (Leung, 2009). ICT connectedness can have both positive and negative consequences in the workplace, which in turn impacts individuals' productivity (Venkatesh, Bala & Sykes, 2010). ICT connectedness allows immediate access to information that influences decision-making (Davis, 2002; Venkatesh, Bala, & Sykes, 2010).

In contrast, an excessive volume of information facilitated by the use of ICT can increase job burnout (Leung, 2011) and stress thus, affect employee productivity in a negative way (Ayyagari, Grover & Purvis, 2011; Hung, Chang & Lin, 2011). Usage of these communication technologies has been increased and so the people are regularly facing some or more problems, but they are continuously neglecting it, research have shown that it is not the problems of academicians only, but of each and every people who come in contact with communication technologies at the workplace or at home or anywhere else, hence, it is a step to explore that do the academicians come to face such kind of problem in Lucknow city of Uttar Pradesh.

## Research Methodology

An exploratory research is conducted and convenience sampling technique is used. A self-structured open ended questionnaire is made based on previous research. The questionnaire comprises 11 questions and personal information. 60 questionnaires were circulated among academicians (20 among higher education educators, 20 among secondary education educators and 20 among primary education educators). The respondents were from Lucknow City only, but as the time frame was limited so respondents are limited to few places only.

## Data Analysis

The questionnaire was circulated among 60 academicians; personal information was asked such as Name, Age, and Class they teach, Mobile Number etc. The problem was that the teachers were not ready to provide their personal information, some provided name, class they teach, age and mobile number, but not all of them answered the full information although it was clearly mentioned to them that the details are only for academic research purpose and it would not be provided to anyone but then also they did not answer.

Out of 60 questionnaire all were answered, but in some questionnaire, few questions were left out by the academicians as blank.

A brief detail of questions are discussed below:

**1. Do you use any communication technology (Smartphone, internet etc.)**

Out of the 60 questionnaires circulated, 100 per cent people answered yes to this question they use internet either by Smartphone or any other device (such as laptop and personal computers).

**2. You use any type of communication technology for approximate how much hours daily or weekly (1-2 hr, 2-3 hr etc. or while using you just do not look-up for time).**

Out of the 60 respondents 10 per cent said they use it just for 30 to 45 minutes daily, 15 per cent said they use it for 1 to 2 hours daily, 55 per cent said they use it for 2 to 3 hours daily, 6 per cent said they use it for 3 to 4 hours, 15 per cent said they use it for 4 to 5 hours daily and 5 per cent said they use it for more than 5 hours.

**3. Constant connectivity might have benefits for some; it also comes at the cost of blurring boundaries between work and home.**

Out of the 60 respondents 45 per cent people replied that Yes. It creates differences between family members, 20 per cent replied that Yes it does take a lot of family time from them, 15 per cent replied that Yes, but boundaries interchange due to importance of work as and when required, 20 per cent only replied yes without stating anything, 5 per cent replied No and 4 per cent did not replied to the question.

**4. Does your significant other ever get frustrated with you because you are spending time at home doing work?**

Out of the 60 respondents 55 per cent of the people replied Yes at times it happens, 45 per cent of the people replied No, never.

**5. Does the constant connectivity due to information and communication technologies ever affect your life in negative way?**

Out of the 60 respondents 65 per cent of the people replied Yes to some extent, 20 per cent of the people replied No, never and 15 per cent replied No, they are careful.

**6. Does your constant connectivity disturb you while you are busy with your work? (Forget where you were as you get distracted or miss something important).**

Out of the 60 respondents 55 per cent of the people replied yes it does affect, 30 per cent of the people replied No, and 15 per cent do not replied at all.

**7. Do you ever feel helpless or lost when these communication technologies gadgets are not with you. (For your phone or validity is not there of you net pack).**

Out of the 60 respondents 30 per cent of the people replied yes always, 20 per cent of the people replied Yes, because certain official notices and calls have to be attended, 15 per cent replied Yes, it does, 10 per cent replied sometimes and 25 per cent replied No.

**8. Do you ever feel that due to the use of the communication technologies you are facing any health problems, (e.g. Fatigue, anxiety, stress, eye-strain, sleep disturbance or any other).**

Out of the 60 respondents 35 per cent of the people replied yes they are facing problem like eyestrain and headache, 25 per cent of the people replied Yes, they feel stressed and sleep disturbance is there, 15 per cent replied they feel pain in the neck part and 20 per cent replied No, they are careful and 5 per cent replied No.

**9. Do you ever feel that while you are busy with these technologies if someone interrupts you get frustrated or say what you were saying?**

Out of the 60 respondents 25 per cent of the people replied yes, sometimes, 30 per cent of the people replied No, never because they give importance to people, 15 per cent of people said No, they do not, they put it down and 15 per cent replied No, they are careful, 10 per cent of people replied No and 5 per cent did not replied anything.

**10. Do you ever feel that when you are free you just go for using these technologies rather than doing anything else (e.g. spending time with family, meeting friends, doing anything creative etc.).**

Out of the 60 respondents 40 per cent of the people replied Yes at times, 20 per cent of the people replied Yes, always and 20 per cent replied No, and 20 per cent replied No, they do not as they do not use them much.

**11. Any other problem you feel that you are facing due to use of these communication technologies.**

Out of the 60 respondents 40 per cent of the people replied

No, 10 per cent of the people do not replied anything. Other people have different views such as few people said taking care of gadgets is an added responsibility, few replied it takes lot of their precious time, few said that they are over dependent on mobile phone, sometime they need to respond which is not needed. Few people said that it is proved to be helpful in updating them, it makes them aware about the surroundings.

## Conclusion

Looking over the above findings it could be clearly concluded that now internet and Smartphone are available nearly with all the educator and the majority of them are using it for 2-3 hours, academicians feel that the usage of communication technologies have left no boundaries between work and home and they faces problem due to it. It is also shown that their significant or family member do get frustrated by their communication technology usage, they feel that their life is being affected in negative way. Academicians feel that their work get affected by the communication technology usage and they feel left out without the communication technology usage whether the reason may be any. The basic problem academician come to face by the use of communication technology are eye-strain, headache, stress and sleep disturbance. Some replied they feel neck pain also.

Academicians do not get frustrated when someone interrupts them while they are using gadgets while only few feel that they face problem. Academicians spend their free time with these gadgets only while they are free as majority agreed. In the case of any other problem they come to face academicians replied their over dependency problems, taking care and some are too much happy as they are being updated by these technology. So, it could be said that on oneside these technologies are helpful on the other they are creating problems we are too much dependent on them and our life and living style is being affected and if so does happen they will not be able to give their 100 per cent to anything whether it may be work or home.

There is a popular saying by Jack Welch *"When the rate of change outside your organization outpaces the rate of change inside your organization, the end is near!"* Few loopholes are there as nothing is perfect in the world it could be suggested that a proper research could be done on this topic by selecting a good time-frame proper population and better sampling technique which was lacking behind, as the sample size was small, convenience sampling technique is used. According to me it could be best resulted when personal interview are taken as if the respondent come to face any problem or unable to understand the question properly the researcher is there to explain them.

## References

Agbonlahor, R.O. (2006). "Motivation for use of information technology by university faculty: a developing country perspective", *Information Development*, Vol. 22, No. 4 : 263-277.

Ayyagari, R. (2012). "Impact of Information overload and task—Technology fit on Technostress", *Proceedings of the Southern Association for Information Systems Conference*, Atlanta, GA, USA, March 23-24.

Ayyagari, R., Grover, V. and Purvis, R.L. (2011). "Technostress: Technology antecedents and implications", *MIS Quarterly*, Vol. 35, No. 4: 831-69.

Brillhart, P.E. (2004) "Technostress in the Workplace: Managing Stress in the Electronic Workplace", *Journal of American Academy of Business*, 5(1/2).

Brod, C. (1984). *Technostress: The Human Cost of the Computer Revolution*. Addison Wesley Publishing.

Davis, G.B. (2002). Anytime/anyplace computing and the future of knowledge work. *Communications of the ACM*, 45(12): 67-73. www.scholarsarchive.jwu.edu

Hung, W.H., Chang, L.M., and Lin, C.H. (2011). *Managing the Risk of Overusing Mobile Phones in the Working Environment: A Study of Ubiquitous Technostress*. Paper presented at the Pacific Asia Conference on Information Systems, Brisbane, Australia.

IAMAI-internet and mobile authority of India, Internet and Mobile 2013, www.imrbint.com

Jarvenpaa, S.L., and Lang, K.R. (2005). Managing the paradoxes of mobile technology. *Information Systems Management*, 22(4): 7-23.

Jenal, R.K. and Mahanti, P.K. (2014). "An Empirical Study of Technostress among Indian Academicians" *International Journal of Education and Learning*, Vol. 3, No. 2: 1-10. www.dx.doi.org

KPMG—cutting through complexity, Mobile India 2014, January 2014, www.comsnets.org

Leung, L. (2009). Effects of Internet connectedness and information literacy on quality of life. *Social Indicators Research,* 98(2): 273-290.

Leung, L. (2011). Effects of ICT Connectedness, Permeability, Flexibility, and Negative Spillovers on Burnout and Job and Family Satisfaction. *Human Technology,* 7(3): 250-267.

Mazmanian, M., Orlikowski, W., and Yates, J.A. (2006). *Crackberries: The Social Implications of Ubiquitous Wireless e-mail Devices.* Paper presented at the EGOS, Bergen.

Odoh, L. and Odigbo, B. (2013). "Effect of Techno-Stress on the Performance of Accountants and Other Managers in Nigerian Banking and Brewery Industries", *European Journal of Business and Management,* Vol. 5, No. 14: 100-108.

Purdy, M., (1997), "The Limits to Human Contact: How Communication Technology Mediates Relationship", Presented International Listening Association Mobile, AL March 13.

Rennecker, J. and Godwin, L. (2003) Individual productivity in this study is thus defined as: *the work accomplished over a unit of time with a given set of resources.*

Rennecker, J., and Godwin, L. (2003). *Theorizing the unintended consequences of instant messaging for worker productivity.* Sprouts: Working Papers on Information Systems. Case Western Reserve University, USA. www.sprouts.aisnet.org

Rosen, L.D. and Weil, M.M. (1998). A Conversation with Technostress, www.technostress.com

Rosen, L.D. and Weil, M.M. (2000a). Four-year study shows more technology work and home but more hesitancy about trying new technology. [Web:] http://www.technostress.com

Rosen, L.D. and Weil, M.M. (2000b). Results of our 49 month study of business attitudes show clerical/support staff, managers and executives using more technology at work and at home and becoming more hesitant toward new technology. www.technostress.com

Tarafdar, M., Tu Q., and Ragu Nathan, T.S. (2010). Impact of technostress on End-User Satisfaction and Performance. *Journal of Management Information Systems,* 27(3): 303-334. www.web.ebscohost.com.

Tarafdar, M., Tu, Q., Ragu Nathan, B.S., and Ragu-Nathan, T. (2007). The impact of technostress on role stress and productivity. *Journal of Management Information Systems,* 24(1): 301-328.

Venkatesh, V., Bala, H., and Sykes, T.A. (2010). Impacts of Information and Communication Technology Implementations on Employees' Jobs in Service Organizations in India: A Multi-Method Longitudinal Field Study, *Production and Operations Management,* 19(5): 591-613.

Vodanovich, S., Sundaram, D., and Myers, M. (2010). Digital natives and ubiquitous information systems. *Information Systems Research,* 21(4): 711-723.

Walz, Katherine, (2012), "Stress Related Issues Due to Too Much Technology: Effects on Working Professionals". *MBA Student Scholarship.* Paper 12.

Weil, M. and Larry, D.R. (1997). Techno-stress: Coping with Technology work home play. New York: John Wiley & Sons, Inc.

www.avendus.com

www.goodreads.com

www.google.co.in

www.60secondmarketer.com

# 10

# Developing Professional Identity

## Technological Aid to Effective Teacher Training Programmes in Higher Education

*Sneha Saha*

Academic identity construction involves different forms of community participation and identification. A professional is someone who has completed a programme of rigorous initial preparation involving specialized knowledge as decided by the profession and who has been approved by the profession as a registered practitioner with the right to exercise autonomous, professional judgement. Most importantly, professionals negotiate the nature of the relationship with members of the public who come to their door. A professional undertakes regular professional updates, is a member of the professional organization reading and contributing to the professional journal and acts in a professional manner according to the established ethical code. Because of their dedication to the field and its participants, professionals are committed to take whatever action they see fit to protect and enhance the manner in which they conduct their work. This is usually done through the aegis of a professional body to which all members of the profession belong. Creating a professional identity is a way to stay current in one's field, open doors of opportunity, and create a lasting impression on those with whom one works. Individuals with a professional identity have control over the initial and long-lasting perceptions people have of them.

**Professional Identity of a Teacher**

Research in higher education has been concentrated on a variety of areas which include the values and collective identities of academic faculty, their role in higher education governance, faculty norms and socialization processes, and the impact of change in higher education on academic roles (Rhoades, 2007). Each discipline has its own concept of success as a vehicle for prestige. Despite these differences, the academic profession possesses a set of common values across disciplinary and institutional boundaries, such as "academic freedom, the community of scholars, scrutiny of accepted wisdom, truth seeking, collegial governance, individual autonomy, and service to society through the production of knowledge, the transmission of culture, and education of the young" (Kuh and Whitt, 1986: 76).

Professional identity for teachers-educators is a constant process of negotiating the many socio-cultural forces, trends and structures within which they work and the relationship they seek to develop with knowledge, with students and their families and with other professional colleagues. Systems of teacher education are described in relation to the structure of the relevant educational systems (stages, duration and main features of these systems), since it is considered that it makes them more intelligible and gives a clearer idea of their fundamental character. A large number of factors determine the calibre of teaching personnel, one of these being the availability of level and quality of institutions for teacher education. Professional identity is also determined by the available teaching equipments (closed-circuit televisions, computer assisted teaching, quality of audio-visual aids). The evaluation of teacher education in terms of its position in the educational system and of the number of years, days and hours required to educate a teacher still represent an approximate approach. To assess an individual's professional worth purely in terms of his/her education at teacher-training programme is a narrow view. It is becoming increasingly necessary to include the work record and experience of every kind in evaluating members of any profession and particularly of teaching profession.

Some years ago, the noted American educator Lee Shulman (1986) proposed a number of teachers' knowledge that all teachers bring into play everyday. These involved curriculum knowledge, subject content knowledge, pedagogical knowledge and general educational knowledge. He pointed out that it is more important for students to develop a depth of understanding of a smaller number of key ideas, rather than to skim across the surface of large tracts of subject content. Shulman also suggested other forms of teacher knowledge such as knowledge of specific cases where students learn or have difficulty in learning and strategic knowledge that enabled different approaches to be used when judged applicable.

According to Beck and Young, Bernstein had located the driving force of professional identity as being centred on the relationship that practitioners have with knowledge, a relationship characterised as 'inwardness' and 'inner dedication'. Bernstein's analysis suggests that professionals operate within a context that includes not only the external conditions of change, but the internal basis of change and that an awareness of the interrelationship between the two at any particular time determines the nature of professional consciousness, commitment and rigour.

> *"In the twenty-first century, students must be fully engaged. This requires the use of technology tools and resources, involvement with interesting and relevant projects, and learning environments including on-line environments—that are supportive and safe.... In the twenty-first century, educators must be given and be prepared to use technology tools; they must be collaborators in learning—constantly seeking knowledge and acquiring new skills along with their students."*
>
> —***Arne Duncan,***
> U.S. Secretary of Education, March 3, 2010

The role of teacher as technician has gained precedence over recent years, with an emphasis on what is called 'teacher quality' (Rowe, 2003). This has come from the 'effective schools' movement where analogous to industry schools are seen as being run by an efficient manager and where 'expert' staff work within the company ideology and direction. Coldron and Smith (1999) found that the professional identity of teachers reflected the landscape that the teacher was a part of that professional identity was manifested in classroom practice and was unique. They also found a tension between agency (the personal dimension in teaching) and structure (the socially given). The structure agency includes the college regulations and various aids available to the teachers.

## Technological Aids to Teaching

In any educational programming, it is essential to take into account such major factors such as objectives, content, methods and materials and evaluation each of them is decisive. Other important factors are the calibre of teachers, the available facilities and aids and the abilities, motivation and social environment of the pupils. Observers, from educators and policy-makers to parents and business people, overwhelmingly agree that technology is an essential component of education. Governments have invested millions to make schools and colleges technology accessible. Yet many schools and colleges remain aloof of basic technology requirement and fail to integrate teaching pedagogy with technological advancements.

The integration of computing, telecommunications, and media-rich information technologies will come to play central roles in the processes of learning and teaching. These vital concerns demand attention from the most rigorous research and theory available, which will contribute the understanding necessary to advance both the practice and sciences of learning. Reports indicated that while beginning teachers may have a theoretical understanding of their role, they were not always 'teacher ready' in terms of the practical experience required. It was noted that improvement in this area could only occur through more participation of pre-service teachers training in schools during their initial preparation. If the education profession is to take such views seriously, that teachers' knowledge is something more than technical rationality and is more holistic knowledge-in-action, then Bernstein's advice (Beck & Young, 2005) regarding the teacher's relationship with knowledge is useful although still in need of greater elaboration.

Earlier, technology in education was a debatable topic amongst the society. Everyone had their own views on modernizing education and making it technology aided. There were a huge number of positives and negatives to education technology. But, gradually as technology was embraced by the educational institutes, they realized the importance of technology in education. Its positives outnumbered the negatives and now, with technology, education has taken a whole new meaning that it leaves us with no doubt that our educational system has been transformed owing to the ever-advancing technology. Technology and education are a great combination if used together with a right reason and vision. Technology is causing education to improve over time. With technology, educators, students and parents have a variety of learning tools at their fingertips. As more students grow-up as digital natives, there is a greater need for educators to adapt to technology changes. Teachers are not trained well enough in how to integrate technology effectively into their classroom, most teachers would say they get thrown technology without having people there to train them. This may be worrisome to some students, who report that technology in the classroom is beneficial to prepare them for the jobs of tomorrow.

Technology is considered to be the wave of the future so, naturally, teachers are encouraged to embrace it. They are encouraged to integrate technology into their lesson plans; they are told that technology is an indispensable tool for learning. Most teachers believe that technology has improved student learning. Giving teachers access to computers, software, and the Internet is only part of incorporating technology successfully into schools. Integrating technology into classrooms depends on the teachers' readiness to use it. If teachers do not feel comfortable with the technology, they are less inclined to incorporate it into their plans. A survey conducted by the National Centre for Education Statistics (NCES) revealed that—

- Among teachers with computers available at home, teachers with the fewest years of experience were more likely than teachers with the most years of experience to use computers or the Internet at home to gather information for planning lessons (76% compared with 63%) and creating instructional materials (91% compared with 82%).
- Teachers cited independent learning most frequently as preparing them for technology use (93%), followed by professional development activities (88%) and their colleagues (87%).

- Teachers indicated that follow-up and advanced training and use of other advanced telecommunications were available less frequently than professional development activities.
- Most teachers said that they had not received the necessary technology training to incorporate technology in their classrooms (NCES, 2000). They need more help. There are several challenges teachers face when trying to embrace technology. Learning new software is just one challenge. Developing lesson plans that incorporate new technology is another challenging issue.
- Modifying traditional teaching techniques to incorporate technology is not easy. It takes time, which teachers often lack. Lack of released time to learn how to use computers and the internet was one of the most frequently reported barriers to public school teachers using computers and the internet in instruction.
- Training, preparation, and work environments also play roles in a teacher's readiness to use technology. Research shows that traditional professional development activities are often short-term, devoid of adequate follow-up, and do not address school contexts. Traditional education programmes for new teachers have been described as "fragmented, superficial, and unconnected to real classroom experiences."

Effective staff development for teachers should take advantage of telecommunication technologies that allow teachers to interact with each other, take on-line courses, and easily access the latest research in their discipline. Teacher professional development in the use of technology should embody and model the forms of pedagogy that teachers can use themselves in their classrooms. To learn how to incorporate technology into their classrooms, teachers should participate in on-line discussion groups, forums, e-mail lists, bulletin boards, message boards, and chat rooms. Technology can promote effective instruction that is more student-centred, inter-disciplinary, more closely related to real-life events and processes, and adaptive to individual learning styles. Such instruction encourages development of higher-order thinking and information-reasoning skills among students, and socially constructed (collaborative) learning, all of which are increasingly required in today's knowledge-based global economy. This potential of technology to improve instruction must be integrated into the design and delivery of teacher professional development programmes in the use of technology. For example, these training programmes should—

- Empower teachers to develop their knowledge and skills actively and experientially, in a variety of learning environments, both individual and collaborative.
- Include a variety of learning strategies, including direct instruction, deduction, discussion, drill and practice, induction and sharing.
- Aim at higher-order thinking skills.
- Provide an authentic learning environment so that teachers engage in concrete tasks within realistic scenarios.
- Emphasize ways that technology can facilitate and enhance teachers' professional lives.
- Encourage teachers to be mentors, tutors and guides of the students' learning process (rather than simple presenters of knowledge and information).
- Develop teachers' skills in learning how to learn (define learning objectives, plan and evaluate learning strategies, monitor progress and adjust as needed).
- Promote cooperative and collaborative learning.
- Be sensitive to the culture and diversity of teachers as learners, using a multifaceted approach so as to respond to different learning styles, opportunities, environments and starting points.
- Enable learning independent of time and place (anytime, anywhere learning).

Perhaps most importantly, technology implies a shift in the teachers' role from being the sole source of knowledge and instruction to being a facilitator of students' learning that is acquired from many sources. This is often referred to as a shift from being "the sage on the stage to the guide on the side." A key for successful teacher professional development programmes is a modular structure, corresponding to different levels of teacher expertise and experience using technology. Adapting materials to teachers' comfort level and starting points is essential. In this way, teachers new to technology can be exposed to the full series of professional development modules, while teachers higher up the learning curve can enter where their knowledge and skills stop, and help their less technology-savvy colleagues along. The basic principles of teacher training programmes should be incorporated, meaning the training programme is highly social and cooperative, with opportunities to share experiences and combine instruction with discussion, reflection, application and evaluation. In addition to these principles, technology enables even more collaborative approach and maximizes peer-to-peer sharing of the challenges, frustrations, advantages and successes of using technology to teach and learn. Such an approach encourages the use of illuminating failures in the use of technology in the classroom, as well as examples of best practice.

It's the teachers who use the technology, not the technology itself, who will be responsible for preparing students for these future jobs. It's up to the people who help the students use technology. If they are good teachers who really help them to learn to use technology, then they will become better students and professionals. But by itself, technology will not make the students better.

## References

Beck, J. and Young, M.F.D. (2005). The assault on the professions and the restructuring of academic and professional identities: a Bernsteinian analysis, *British Journal of Sociology of Education,* 26(2): 183-197.

Coldron, J., and Smith, R. (1999). Active location in teachers' construction of their professional identities. *Journal of Curriculum Studies,* 31(6): 711-726.

Delannoy, Francoise , (2000). "Teacher Training or Lifelong Professional Development," *Tech Know Logia,* November/December.

Guhlin, M. (1996). Stage a well designed Saturday session and they will come! *Technology Connection,* 3(3): 13-14.

Kuh, G.D., and Whitt, E.J. (1986). The invisible tapestry: culture in American colleges and universities (*ASHE-ERIC Higher Education Report, No.* 1). Washington: The George Washington University.

NCES. (2000). *Teacher's Tools for the 21st century*. Washington, D.C.: U.S. Department of Education.

Rowe, K. (2003). The Importance of Teacher Quality as a Key Determinant of Students' Experiences and Outcomes of Schooling, *background paper to keynote address presented at the ACER Research Conference*, Melbourne, October.

Rhoades, G. (2007). The study of the academic profession. In P.J. Gumport (Ed.), *Sociology of Higher Education. Contributions and their Contexts* (pp. 113-146). Baltimore: The Johns Hopkins University Press.

Shulman, L.S. (1986). Those Who Understand Knowledge Growth in Teaching, *Educational Researcher*, 15(2), 4-15.

# 11

# Technological Integration with Teaching Pedagogy

*Sushma*

## Introduction

> *"Books will soon be obsolete in the public schools; our school system will be completely changed inside of ten years."*
>
> **—*Thomas Edison***

It is the need of the hour that educators must perceive technology in education as part of the pedagogical process. It is necessary for teachers to understand the pedagogical principles that govern the application of technology into teaching and learning. Educators are encouraged to view technology integration from a wider perspective and be reflective in their teaching as they use technology to support and facilitate instruction.

Advancements in IT have revolutionized the process of communication as well as learning, but technology has failed to transform the practical aspects of education system yet now. The problem of integrating technology into teaching and learning process has become a perennial one. Common excuses for the limited use of technology to support instruction include shortage of computers, lack of computer skill and computer intimidation. While these could affect the success of technology integration, it should be acknowledged that the degree of success teachers using technology for instruction could depend in part on their ability to explore the relationship between pedagogy and technology. To overcome these obstacles, it is required to persuade teachers that technology will empower them and help their students learn. Some pedagogical principles must be followed in this process:

(a) ***Educational Institutions Must Use Technology to Empower Teachers***: The present era of technology had made almost all information in the reach of every child. Social media platforms like Twitter, Facebook etc. have enabled dynamic communication with students. Teacher-empowering technologies include mobile apps that provide lesson plan databases. Education systems need to aggressively track to check what works for their teachers and what not.

(b) ***Technology as Part of Lesson Plan***: Lesson plans must be inherited with the use of technology in order to increase effectiveness. It also helps to manage in all constraints as well.

(c) ***Teachers Should Not Fear to Use Open-Source Technologies***: It is generally assumed that technologies are expensive and complicated to use, however, open-source technologies are stable, secure, and compatible with other platforms. These platforms often have large communities that provide high quality customer support system.

(d) ***Use of Online Portfolios to Evaluate Students***: Educators should understand the benefits of on-line portfolios for new generations as it allows students to express creativity. Teachers can choose from a variety of on-line portfolio providers as they cost less and allow for more robust outreach. Online portfolios are also amenable to a wider variety of formats including video, music or other interactive features.

(e) ***Teachers Should Embrace the Core Standards***: The use of technology should not compromise with variations from the core and fixed set standards. There should be universally acceptable standard for all institutes by the governing body (like UGC or AICTE) as common standards make teaching simpler. Universal adoption of common standards will support future technological innovations that will aid teachers.

**Literature Review**

Draude *et al.*, (1998) in their study "Assessing the Impact of Technology on Teaching and Learning: Student Perspectives" assessed the impact of technology on teaching and learning. For this a four-part questionnaire was distributed to 1,900 students in technology-equipped classrooms across campus. The first part of the questionnaire measured student perceptions and skills related to various types of technologies. The second part measured frequency of use of various instructional technology applications, including computer applications to present lecture outlines or demonstrate concepts, audio/visual equipment, electronic communication, and supplementary use or development of materials such as World Wide Web pages, computer-assisted instruction modules, and computer-based applications. The third segment of the questionnaire gathered information about the projected future use of instructional technology by students, and the final portion gathered demographic information. Survey results led to the following major findings:

- Use of instructional technology positively affects student learning.
- Use of instructional technology increases student interest and satisfaction.
- Role of faculty and their ability to use instructional technology are major factors.
- Certain instructional technology techniques better facilitate certain learning activities.
- Instructional technology is an integral part of today's learning environment.

Bates *et al.*, in their study "Effective Teaching with Technology in Higher Education: Foundations for Success" provides a theoretical and pedagogical foundation for helping instructors make critical decisions about the use of technology within the college curriculum. It discusses the relationship between knowledge, learning, teaching, and the nature of media, and shows how this information should inform the use of technology in a teaching environment. They also provide guidance for developing and delivering a course using electronic technology and discuss the organizational and technical support structures that are needed to back-up instructors using technology.

According to Mizell *et al.* (2005) "Educational technology might include media, models, projected and non-projected visual, as well as audio, video and digital media. These authors claimed that some educators may take a narrower view and are likely to confine educational technology primarily to computers, computer peripherals and related software used for teaching and learning."

Weizenbaum (1976) argues that "Computers can be a powerful metaphor for understanding many aspects of the world." However, he states "It enslaves the mind that has no metaphors and few resources to call on the mind that has been educated with only facts and skills" (p. 51). It is important that practicing teachers and in-service teachers recognize that technology in education is considered as the part of pedagogy.

Topper (2005) believes that "For teachers to use technology in support of their teaching, and to see it as a pedagogically useful tool, they must be confident and competent with the technology they are planning to use" (p. 304).

The words of Alfred Kyle, Dean of Engineering, are very insightful in discussing critical and reflective teaching (Schon, 1987). He mentioned, "We know how to teach people to build ships, but not how to figure out what ships to build" (p. 11). It is hoped that instructors will develop similar awareness by becoming critical thinkers and reflective teachers as they engage in technology integration.

Pierson (2001) recognized that, "Society has embraced computer technology and allowed it to reinvent the ways in which we create, find, exchange, and even think about information. Unable to ignore such deeply permeating innovation, school districts often bow to societal pressure to fund technology, without having a thoughtful plan for implementation" (p. 413).

Payal Mehra and Monika Mittal (2007) in their study "Integrating technology into the teaching-learning transaction: Pedagogical and technological perceptions of management faculty", revealed that new age technology teaching was partly intimidating. A large population found it easier to prepare lectures on transparencies rather than use the computer. Most of them also felt that instructional technology was highly training intensive and they needed guidance for using instructional technology as a teaching Aid. Many faculty members felt that given a choice they would still prefer to use the lecture method for effective instruction in class. But on a positive note they also felt that they had more time to devote to intellectual enhancements as instructional technology has resulted in saving time for the respondents. Only a small percentage believed that instructional technology was more easily adopted by faculty who had IT/Engineering background.

A very large population was of the strong belief that effectiveness of the lectures is still person oriented and not technology oriented, given the flux of technology enabled teaching environment in the country today. An Overwhelming majority felt that instructional technology enhanced their global orientation as it exposed the faculty to the best practices in the rest of the world.

**The TPACK Framework**

The Technological Pedagogical Content Knowledge (TPACK) framework of Shulman (1987) provides description of PCK (Pedagogical Content Knowledge) to create understanding of how teachers' knowledge of educational technologies and PCK to produce effective teaching with technology. Various authors have discussed same idea, though often using different labelling. The conception of TPACK described here has developed over time and through a series of publications, with the most complete descriptions of the framework found in Koehler and Mishra (2008) (*See* Fig. 11.1).

In this model, there are three main components: teachers' knowledge, content pedagogy and technology and also the interactions between and among these bodies of knowledge, represented as Pedagogical Content Knowledge (PCK), Technological Content Knowledge (TCK ) and Technological Pedagogical Knowledge (TPK), and TPACK. Content knowledge (CK) is teachers' knowledge about the subject matter to be learned or taught. Pedagogical knowledge (PK) is teachers' deep knowledge about the processes and practices or methods of teaching and learning. They encompass, among other things, overall educational purposes, values, and aims. PCK covers the core business of teaching, learning, curriculum, assessment and reporting, such as the conditions that promote learning and the links among

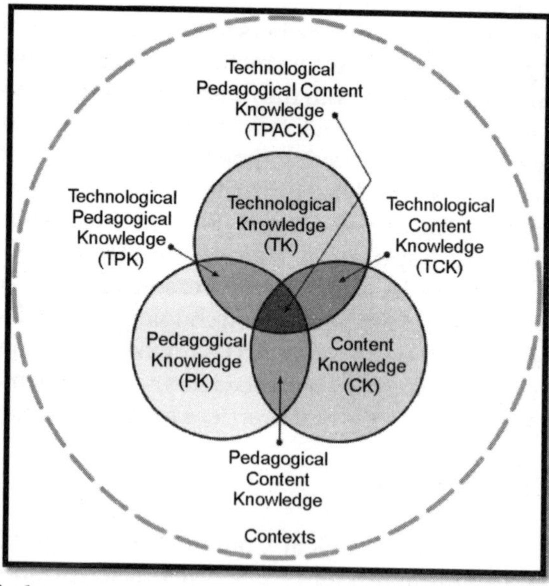


*Source:* Shulman (1987).

**Fig. 11.1:** The TPACK Framework

curriculum, assessment, and pedagogy. TCK is an understanding of the manner in which technology and content influence and constrain one another.

The TPACK framework offers several possibilities for promoting research in teacher education, teacher professional development, and teachers' use of technology. It offers options for looking at a complex phenomenon like technology integration in ways that are now amenable to analysis and development. Moreover, it allows teachers, researchers, and teacher educators to move beyond oversimplified approaches that treat technology as an "add-on" instead to focus again, and in a more ecological way, upon the connections among technology, content, and pedagogy as they play out in classroom contexts.

## Use of Technology in Education and Teaching Pedagogy

Technological integration is a complex process and is made-up of various interconnected activities. A major part of the problem related to technology integration is that most educators have not addressed the pedagogical principles that will guide their use of technology for teaching and learning. The intricate relationship between technology and pedagogy has not been adequately explored. As teachers explore the process of technology integration and search for ways that it can be effectively accomplished, they will develop the rationale to examine the appropriateness of the technologies they are using and whether such technologies are compatible with their lesson plan and learning outcomes or not. The process of exploring the relationship between technology in education and pedagogy will encourage critical thinking on the part of teachers as they practice technology integration. Still there are some critical areas that need to be evaluated and followed:

- Identify learning objectives that requires teachers to select or adapt technology to match the students' needs.
- Technology selection, learning styles, modes and pace of learning using technology as part of the instructional process requires teachers to choose the methods that are relevant to the objectives.
- Evaluation of selected techniques that are relevant to the objectives aimed.
- Develop follow-up techniques that are accessible to the students and also easy to use.
- Designing course enrichment materials using technology requires teachers to provide opportunity for students to explore issues that broaden their problem-solving skiils.
- Designing a dynamic classroom using technology requires teachers to provide a learning environment that is engaging, exciting, interactive and energetic.

## Conclusion

Technological integration is narrowly perceived and that such a perception might hinder teacher understanding of the scope of technology in education. Technology integration should be considered along with issues involved in teaching and learning. Such issues include developing learning objectives, selecting methods of instruction, feedback, and evaluation and assessment strategies including follow-up activities. Technology used for teaching and learning should be considered an integral part of instruction and not as an object exclusive to itself. Viewing technology integration from a wide perspective will provide teachers with the necessary foundation to implement technology into the classroom more successfully.

Technology should be implemented in the classroom only if its role in a given instruction is determined along with pedagogical issues related to a given instructional task. The role of technology in education can only be determined if teachers who implement technology at the classroom level are involved in technology decision-making because teachers have the responsibility of facilitating instruction. It is important that teachers recognize that a relationship exists between technology in education and pedagogical decision-making.

## References

Anderson, C.L. and Borthwick, A. (2002). *Results of separate and integrated technology instruction in pre-service training*. ERIC Reproduction Document, p. 14.

Ausubel, D.P. (1978). *Educational Psychology: A Cognitive View.* (2nd ed.). New York: Holt, Rinehart & Winston.

Bazeli, M. (1997). Visual productions and student learning. ERIC Reproduction. Fall Bosch, K.A. and Cardinale, L. (1993). Preservice teacher' perceptions of computer use during a field experience. *Journal of Computing in Teacher Education,* 10(1), pp. 23-27.

Diaz, D.P. and Bontenbal, K.F. (2000). Pedagogy-based technology training. In P. Hoffman and D. Lemke (eds.), *Teaching and Learning in a Network World,* pp. 50-54. Amsterdam, Netherlands: 105 Press.

Draude *et al.* (1998), "Assessing the Impact of Technology on Teaching and Learning: Student Perspectives", *International Journal of Education and Development using Information and Communication Technology (IJEDICT),* 2012, Vol. 8, Issue 1, pp. 136-155.

Eby, J. (1997). *Reflective Planning, Teaching and Evaluation, K-12.* Upper Saddle River, NJ: Prentice Hall.

Fletcher, G. (1996). Former Director of the Division of Educational Technology, Texas Education Agency, Executive Vice President of T.H.E. Institute quoted in *T.H.E. Journal,* 24(4), p. 87.

Gess-Newsome, J., Blocher, M., Clark, J., Menasco, J., and Willis, E. (2003). Technology infused professional development: A framework for development and analysis. *Contemporary Issues in Technology and Teacher Education,* 3(3), pp. 324-340.

Gunter, S.C. (2002). *Integrating Technology in the Classroom.* Canada: Thompson: Learning.

Jonassen, D.H. (ed.) (2004). *Handbook of Research on Educational Communications and Technology.* Lawrence Erlbaum Associates, Publishers: Mahwah, New Jersey.

Koehler, M.J., and Mishra, P. (2009), "What is Technological Pedagogical Content Knowledge?", *Michigan State University, Contemporary Issues in Technology and Teacher Education,* 9(1). Retrieved from http://www.citejournal.org

Leh, A.S. (2005). Learned from service learning and reverse mentoring in faculty development: A case study in technology training. *Journal of Technology and Teacher Education,* 13(1), pp. 25-41.

Lever-Duffy, J. McDonald, J.B. and Mizell Al P. (2005). *Teaching and Learning with Technology.* San Francisco: Pearson.

Mann, D. (1999). Documenting the Effects of Instructional Technology: A Fly-over of Policy Questions. http://www.ed.gov/Technology/TechCont/1999/whitepapers/paper6.html

McGrail, E. (2005). Teachers, Technology and change: English teachers perspectives. *Journal of Technology and Teacher Education,* 13(13), pp. 5-23.

Means, B. (1994). Introduction: Using technology to advance educational goals. In B. Means (Ed.), *Technology and Education Reform: The Reality Behind the Promise,* pp. 1-21. San Francisco: Jossey-Bass.

Mehra, P. and Mittal M. (2007). "Integrating technology into the teaching-learning transaction: Pedagogical and technological perceptions of management faculty", *International Journal of Education and Development using Information and Communication Technology* (IJEDICT), Vol. 3, Issue 1, pp. 105-115.

Mezirow, J. (1990). *Fostering Critical Reflection in Adulthood: A guide to transformative and empanicipatory learning.* San Francisco: Jossey-Bass.

Okojie, Mabel CPO, Olinzock, A.A. and Okojie-Boulder, T.C. (2005). *Technology Training Dilemma: A Diagnostic Approach,* An unpublished manuscript.

Pierson, M. (2001). Technology integration practice as a function of pedagogical experts. *Journal of Research on Computing in Education,* 33(5).

Ripley, D. (2001). Using technology to foster critical thinking and reflection: The R9 process. *International Journal of Vocational Education and Training,* 9(2), November.

Schon, D. (1990). *The Reflective Practitioner: How Professionals Think in Action.* New York: Basic Books.

Sprague, D., Kopfman, K. and Dorsey, S. (1998). Faculty development in the integration of technology in teacher education courses. *Journal of Computing in Teacher Education,* 2(14), pp. 24-28. *The American Heritage*

*Dictionary of English Language* (3rd edition). Boston, MA: Houghton Mifflin Company.

Topper, A. (2004). How are we doing? Using self-assessment to measure changing teacher technology literacy within a graduate education technology programme, 12(3), pp. 303-317.

Weizenbaum, J. (1976), *Computer Power and Human Reason*, San Francisco, CA: W.H. Freeman.

Yao, J., Ouyang, J. and Wang H. (2000). A farewell to the traditional instructional media and technologies in the new millennium. Society for Information Technology and Teacher Education International Conference, February 8-12.

http://www.brookings.edu (accessed in August 2015)

http://www.theguardian.com (accessed in August 2015)

http://cft.vanderbilt.edu (accessed in August 2015)

# 12

# E-Learning and Its Effects on Teaching and Learning in Urban Age

*Meenakshi Dwivedi*

## Introduction

Mankind has entered the urban age. When it comes to education, the model has been pretty straight forward-up until the early education was in a classroom where students with a teacher-led the process. Physical presence was a no-brainer, and any other type of learning was questionable at best. Then the computer evolution happened and it radically changed the learning landscape.

E-learning is a computer based educational tool or system that enables you to learn anywhere and at any time. Today E-learning is mostly delivered through the internet, although in the past it was delivered using a blend of computer-based methods like CD-ROM. Technology has advanced so much that the geographical gap is bridged with the use of tools that make us feel as if we are inside the classroom. E-learning offers the ability to share material in all kinds of formats such as videos, slideshows, word documents and PDFs. Conducting webinars (live on-line classes) and communicating with professors *via* chat and message forums is also an option available to users.

E-learning can be defined as an approach to teaching and learning that utilizes Internet technologies to communicate and collaborate in an educational context. This includes technology that supplements traditional classroom training with web-based components and learning environments where the educational process is experienced on-line.

E-learning according to Markus (2008) can be defined as a learning process created by interaction with digitally delivered content, network-based services and tutoring support. E-learning is any technologically mediated learning using computers whether from a distance or in face-to-face classroom setting (computer assisted learning), it is a shift from traditional education or training to ICT-based personalized, flexible, individual, self-organized, collaborative learning-based on a community of learners, teachers, facilitators, and experts. E-learning is the use of Internet technologies to enhance knowledge and performance. E-learning technologies offer learners control over content, learning sequence, pace of learning, time, and often media, allowing them to tailor their experiences to meet their personal learning objectives to manage access to E-learning materials, consensus on technical standardization, and methods for peer review of these resources. E-learning presents numerous research opportunities for faculty, along with continuing challenges for documenting scholarship. Innovations in E-learning technologies point towards a revolution in education, allowing learning to be individualized (adaptive learning), enhancing learners' interactions with others (collaborative learning), and transforming the role of the teacher. The integration of E-learning into education can catalyze the shift towards applying adult learning theory, where educators will no longer serve mainly as the distributors of content, but will become more involved as facilitators of learning and assessors of competency.

In some definitions E-Learning encompasses more than just the offering of wholly on-line courses. For instance Oblinger and Hawkins (2005) noted that E-Learning has transformed from a fully-on-line course to using technology to deliver part or all of a course independent of permanent time and place. Also the European Commission (2001) describes, E-Learning as the use of new multimedia technologies and the Internet to increase learning quality by easing access to facilities and services as well as distant exchanges and collaboration.

E-learning refers to the use of information and communication technologies to enable the access to on-line learning/teaching resources. In its broadest sense, Abbad *et al.* (2009), defined

E-learning to mean any learning that is enabled electronically. They, however, narrowed this definition down to mean learning, that is empowered by the use of digital technologies. This definition is further narrowed by some researchers as any learning that is internet-enabled or web-based (LaRose *et al.*, 1998; Keller and Cernerud, 2002).

## Components of E-Learning

Creating E-learning material involves several components. Once content is developed, it must be managed, delivered, and standardized. Content comprises all instructional material, which can range in complexity from discrete items to larger instructional modules. A digital learning object is defined as any grouping of digital materials structured in a meaningful way and tied to an educational objective.

Learning objects represent discrete, self-contained units of instructional material assembled and reassembled around specific learning objectives, which are used to build larger educational materials such as lessons, modules, or complete courses to meet the requirements of a specified curriculum. Examples include: tutorials, case-based learning, hypermedia, simulations, and game based learning modules. Content creators use instructional design and pedagogical principles to produce learning objects and instructional materials. Content management includes all the administrative functions (e.g., storing, indexing, cataloguing) needed to make E-learning content available to learners. Examples include portals, repositories, digital libraries, learning-management systems, search engines, and E-Portfolios.

## Synchronous or Asynchronous Delivery of Content

There are fundamentally two types of E-Learning:

- Synchronous training
- Asynchronous training

Synchronous means "at the same time," involves interaction of participants with an instructor *via* the Web in real time. For example—Virtual classrooms (VCRs) that are nothing else but real classrooms on-line. Participants interact with each other and instructors through instant messaging, chat, audio- and video-conferencing etc. and what's more all the sessions can be recorded and played back. Synchronous delivery refers to real-time, instructor-led E-learning, where all learners receive information simultaneously and communicate directly with other learners. Examples include teleconferencing (audio, video, or both), Internet chat forums, and instant messaging. Its benefits are:

- Ability to log or track learning activities.
- Continuous monitoring and correction is possible.
- Possibilities of global connectivity and collaboration opportunities among learners.
- Ability to personalise the training for each learner.

Asynchronous, which means "not at the same time," allows the participants to complete the WBT (Web-based training) at their own pace, without live interaction with the instructor. Basically, it is information that is accessible on a self-help basis, 24/7. The advantage is that this kind of e-Learning offers the learners the information they need whenever they need it. It also has interaction amongst participants through message boards, bulletin boards and discussion forums. These include computer based training (CBTs) modules on CD-Roms, Web based training accessed through intranet (WBTs) or through well written articles and other write ups. In asynchronous delivery, the transmission and receipt of information do not occur simultaneously. The learners are responsible for facing their own self-instruction and learning. The instructor and learners communicate using e-mail or feedback technologies, but not in real time. A variety of methods can be used for asynchronous delivery, including e-mail, on-line bulletin boards, newsgroups, and Weblogs. Its advantages are:

- Available 'just in time' for instant learning and reference.
- Flexibility of access from anywhere at any time.
- Ability to simultaneously reach an unlimited number of employees.
- Uniformity of content and onetime cost of production.

A new form of learning known as blended learning is

emerging. As the name suggests it is an amalgamation of synchronous and asynchronous learning methods. Using both on-line training through virtual classrooms and also giving CDs and study material for self-study is now being increasingly preferred over any single type of training.

## Blended Learning

Blended learning is a combination of off-line (face-to-face, traditional learning) and on-line learning in a way that the one compliments the other. It provides individuals with the opportunity to enjoy the best of both worlds. For example, a student might attend classes in a real-world classroom setting, and then supplement the lesson plan by completing on-line multimedia coursework. As such, the student would only have to physically attend class once a week and would be free to go at their own pace (and without worrying about scheduling issues). Blended learning is often also referred to as "hybrid" learning, and can take on a variety of forms in on-line education environments. While some organizations may only use blended learning techniques on rare occasions, others might utilize it as a primary teaching method within their curriculum.

There are two key principles commonly associated with blended learning, which are the secrets to its success. First the students who can share information and work with other students directly in a collaborative setting have a more enriched learning experience, and second collaboration between students can be improved upon if group activities rely on information gathered from on-line resources or lessons. It has also been suggested that students who complete on-line coursework followed by interactive, face-to-face class activities have richer educational experiences.

## How to Make E-Learning More Effective

We can easily make the E-learning more effective, but for this we need:

- Availability of good quality hardware (particularly computers).

- Availability of faster internet connectivity/improved bandwidth.
- Improved quality secured software.
- Appropriate government policies favouring E-learning.
- Provision of technical support for E-learning at a range of scales.
- Lower prices for connectivity.
- Availability of reliable electricity.
- Availability and development of appropriate content in appropriate languages.
- Raising the level of awareness about the value of E-learning.
- Improved training for teachers in E-learning at all levels.

**Benefits of E-learning**

- E-learning is important because it can improve the quality of the learning experience, and extend the reach of every lecturer and tutor.
- E-learning can help remove barriers to achievement, by providing new and creative ways of motivating and engaging pupils and learners of all abilities, enabling and inspiring everyone to attain their educational potential.
- E-learning can support learning by offering differentiated learning, particularly for those who need support in literacy, numeracy and ICT.
- E-learning offers a wide range of tools to enable teachers and learners to be innovative, creative and resourceful in all learning activities. Teachers and learners can easily customize digital learning resources to suit pace and level, appropriate to any learning style and ability.
- E-learning creates on-line communities of practice. The Internet can bring learners, teachers, specialist communities, experts, practitioners and interest groups together to share ideas and good practice.
- E-learning can provide an individualized learning experience for all learners, including those who are disadvantaged, disabled, exceptionally gifted, have special curriculum or learning needs or who are remote or away from their usual place of learning.

- E-learning can facilitate wider participation and fairer access to further education by creating the opportunity to start learning and to choose courses and support according to the learners' needs.
- E-learning provides personalized learning support through information, advice, and guidance services. It can help learners find the course they need, with a seamless transition to the next stage of their learning, including on-line application or enrollment and an electronic portfolio of their learning to take with them.
- E-learning provides virtual learning worlds where learners can take part in active and creative learning with others through simulations, role-play, remote control of real world tools and devices, on-line master classes, or collaboration with other education providers.
- E-learning enhances the efficacy of knowledge and qualifications *via* ease of access to a huge amount of information.
- E-learning is cost effective in the sense that there is no need for the students or learners to travel. It is also cost effective in the sense that it offers opportunities for learning for maximum number of learners with no need for many buildings.
- E-learning helps compensate for scarcities of academic staff, including instructors or teachers as well as facilitators, lab technicians etc.
- The use of e-Learning allows self-pacing. For instance the asynchronous way permits each student to study at his or her own pace and speed whether slow or quick. It, therefore, increases satisfaction and decreases stress.

## Personalization and E-learning

Personalized Learning is the tailoring of pedagogy, curriculum and learning environments to meet the needs and learning styles of individual learners. Personalization is broader than just individualization or differentiation in that it affords the learner a degree of choice about what is learned, when it is learned and how it is learned.

In essence, personalized e-learning enables students to

customize a variety of the elements involved in the on-line education process. This means that they are asked to set their own goals, go at their own pace, and communicate with instructors and students to personalize the learning process. Ideally, the student is placed in charge of managing his/her own learning and is able to customize the experience by having a direct say in the processes and content that is being provided. Key elements that are customized in personalized E-learning are: the pace of learning, the instructional approach, and lessons and activities that draw upon the student's experience and interests. In truly personalized e-learning environments students are given the chance to learn what they want when they want, and even the method of learning. This typically leads to improved learning results.

## Conclusion

The integration of web-based learning components with software like 'Course Info' bring added value to traditional education. Students and faculty benefit from using the communication and assessment tools. Students have a customized approach to knowledge acquisition that suits learning styles and busy schedules. Continual access to resources through on-line delivery and automated management tools minimizes the faculty's cost and time associated with the experience. The advantages of E-learning make a significant impact on education today and, as technology evolves, promise to deliver even greater benefits in the future.

## References

Abbad, M.M., Morris, D., and de Nahlik, C. (2009). Looking under the Bonnet: Factors Affecting Student Adoption of E-Learning Systems in Jordan. *The International Review of Research in Open and Distance Learning*.

Collins, J., Hammond, M. and Wellington, J. (1997). *Teaching and Learning with Multimedia*, London: Routledge.

European Commission (2001). The eLearning Action Plan: Designing tomorrow's education. http://www.elearningeuropa.info.

Keller, C. and Cernerud, L. (2002). Students' perception of e-learning in university education. *Learning, Media and Technology*, 27(1), 55-67.

Klein, D. and Ware, M. (2003). E-learning: new opportunities in continuing professional development. *Learned Publishing*, 16 (1), 34-46.

LaRose, R., Gregg, J., and Eastin, M. (1998). Audio graphic tele-courses for the Web: An experiment. *Journal of Computer Mediated Communications*, 4(2).

Pagram, P., and Pagram, J., (2006). "Issues in e-learning: A Thai Case Study", *The Electronic Journal of Information Systems in Developing Countries*, Vol. 26, No. 6. 1-8.

Oblinger, D.G., and Hawkins, B.L. (2005). The myth about E-learning. *Educause review*.

Rossi, P.G. (2009). Learning environment with artificial intelligence elements. *Journal of e-learning and knowledge society*, 5(1), 67-75.

Rosenberg, J.M. (2001). *E-learning: Strategies for Delivering Knowledge* in the Digital Age. McGraw-Hill: New York.

Wood, R., and Ashfield, J. (2008). The use of the interactive whiteboard for creative teaching and learning in literacy and mathematics: a case study. *British Journal of Educational Technology*, 39 (1), 84-96.

# 13

# Application of Multimedia Technology in Modern Teaching

*Archana Jha*

## Introduction

Multimedia by definition means "more than one media". Multimedia approach means the use of teaching material in different forms in order to clarify a topic. In other words, using the communication medium along with instructional methods and techniques is called multimedia approach. Here, multimedia does not meant the use of many media, but planned used of many media and techniques. In the words of Dr. Bhoraskar: "Multimedia approach means the maximum utilization of effectiveness of different techniques and media in proper combination to achieve the desired end." In teaching, multimedia approach is also called instructional development. This is used for educational, recreational and effective expression. This approach performs all functions related to information, instruction, enrichment, recreation and persuasion.

The development of multimedia technologies for learning offers new ways in which learning can take place in schools and the home. Enabling teachers to have access to multimedia learning resources, supports constructive concept development which allows the teacher to focus more on being a facilitator of learning while working with individual students. Extending the use of multimedia learning resources to the home represents an educational opportunity with the potential to improve student learning. Multimedia simply combines elements into a powerful new tool, especially in the hands of teachers and students.

Interactive multimedia weaves five basic types of media into the learning environment: text, video, sound, graphics and animation. Since the mode of learning is interactive and not linear a student or a teacher can choose what to investigate next. For example, one does not start on the first page of a linear document and read to the end. Interactive multimedia learning mode is more like constructing a spider's web, with one idea linked to another, allowing choices in the learner's path. The element of multimedia in Education is very tempting to use the latest computer wizard to represent information and develop computer enhanced learning material. However, the instructional design of these systems should be based on a careful examination and analysis of the many factors, both human and technical, relating to visual learning.

When is sound more meaningful than a picture? How much text is too much? Students must be able to select appropriate multimedia tools and apply them to learning task within the learning environment in order to effective learning to take place. A multimedia learning environment involves a number of components or elements in order to enable learning to take place. Hardware and software are the only part of the requirement. Multimedia learning integrates five types of media to provide flexibility in expressing the creativity of the student and exchanging ideas out of all the elements, text has the great impact on the quality of the multimedia interaction. Text provides the important information. Text acts as the keystone lying all of the other media elements together. It is well written text that makes a multimedia communication wonderful. Digital texts can be read aloud using recorded human voice or synthetic text-to-speech programmes. Readaloud is an intrinsic feature of so-called talking books, but with text to speech software, vitality any digital content—including web-based texts—can be read aloud, with or without synchronous highlighting of the printed text.

Speech synthesis can be segmented at a variety of levels, providing feedback at the level of the passage, sentence, word, onset rime, syllable or sub-syllable. Read-aloud offers potential benefits to many students including students with visual deficits, students with decoding problems, and reluctant readers. In addition to providing access to curriculum content for those who cannot see or decode printed text, read-aloud can support the development of key literacy skills such as fluency and reading comprehension, and increase engagement and motivation. Text-to-speech is also a beneficial writing tool. It may be easier for students to recognize errors when listening *versus* reading a composition. By using text-to-speech to read back the text they have written material, students may be able to revise more successfully.

Sound is used to provide emphasis or highlight a transition from one page to another. Sound synchronized to screen display, enables teachers to present lots of information at once. This approach is used in a variety of ways, all based on visual display of a complex image paired with a spoken explanation.

Video—The representation of information by using the visualization capabilities of video can be immediate and powerful. It is the ability to choose how we view, and interact with the content of digital video that provides new and exciting possibilities for the use of digital video in education. Video can be used to give examples of phenomena or issues referred to in the text. Video needs to be used to supplement textual information. The use of video is appropriate to convey information about environments that can be either dangerous or too costly to consider, or recreate, in life. Animation is used to show changes in state over time, or to present information slowly to students, so, they have time to assimilate in smaller chunks. Animation, when combined with user input, enables students to view different versions of changes over time, depending on different variables. Animations are primarily used to demonstrate an idea or illustrate a concept. There are two types of animation: Cell-based and Object-based animation. Cell-based animation consist of multiple drawings, each one a little different from the others.

## Multimedia in Teaching-Learning

Multimedia approach has unique importance in the educational system and social transactions. It has played an important role in innovation and improvement in teaching methods, individualization of instruction and an effective learning system for a fairly large number of students:

- Multimedia approach in teaching and learning is

psychologically sound. Variety and newness of the media motivate the students for learning both at the preparation and participation stages and promote learning. Students are benifited from recreational activities like pictures, charts, posters, models, stories and plays, accounts of travels and musical productions.

- Multimedia approach in teaching and learning is essential for the effective realization of learning objectives and also provides learning environment in which students take active part in the learning process.
- Multimedia approach in teaching and learning is learner-centred in the sense that it can accommodate learner's needs and interests. The variety and flexibility of multimedia offer the opportunity to adopt any media combination for use in individualized instruction.
- Various types of media like computer, television, video cassettes, video discs etc. can be of great value in supplementing and enriching the class-room instruction.
- Media like audio cassettes and CDs enable the learners to receive any given information according to their own convenient time.

A multimedia learning environment involves a number of components or elements in order to enable learning to take place. Multimedia learning integrates five types of media to provide flexibility in expressing the creativity of student and in exchanging ideas out of all the elements, text has the most important impact on the quality of the multimedia interaction.

## Importance of Multimedia

In terms of the delivery medium, the educator can deliver the message *via* the 'chalk and talk' method and overhead projector. The directed instruction model is a popular technique, which has been used for decades as an educational strategy in all institution of learning. Basically, the teacher controls the instructional process, the content is delivered to the entire class and the teacher tends to emphasize factual knowledge. In other words, the teacher delivers the lecture content and the students listen to the lecture. Thus, the learning mode tends to be passive and the learners play a little part in their learning process.

Some limitations which may prevail in traditional teaching methods are:

- Teaching in classroom using chalk and talk is 'one way flow' of information.
- Teachers often continuously talk for an hour without knowing students response and feedback.
- The material presented is only based on lecture notes and textbooks.
- There is insufficient interaction with students in classroom.
- More emphasis has been given on theory without any practical and real life-time situations.
- Learning from memorization but not understanding.
- Marks rather than result oriented.

In order to solve the problem, multimedia can be effectively used for instructional purposes. Further, Cairncross and Mannion (2001) pointed out that multimedia has the potential to create high quality learning environment. The key elements of multiple media, user control over the delivery of information, and interactivity can be used to enhance the learning process creating integrated learning environment.

Multimedia is also fast emerging as a basic skill that will be as important to life in the twenty-first century as reading. In fact, multimedia is changing the nature of reading itself. Instead of limiting us to the linear presentation of text, multimedia makes reading dynamic by expanding the text in certain topics. This is accomplished not only by providing more text but by bringing it to life with sound, pictures, music and video. Integration of multimedia into instruction can help to reduce curriculum barriers and improve learning for all students.

**Need and Characteristics of Multimedia Approach**

- The multimedia approach is a good tool to meet the increasing demand of education for the fulfilment of student's educational needs, as per their ability and make the course material comprehensible.

- The use of multimedia approach motivates a student for learning, and it makes the teaching-learning process interesting.
- The use of multimedia approach makes the content clearer and comprehensible.
- A teacher can use the multimedia approach in order to explain difficult and complicated concept in an easy manner and thus saves his time and energy.
- The concepts taught by the multimedia approach are clearer and comprehensible to students, so that students do not have to learn them by rote.
- The use of multimedia approach helps to retain learning more permanently.
- The multimedia approach can keep better control over the learners; they can practice as per their own need and can examine their progress.

## Educational Benefits of Multimedia Tools from the Educator's Perspective

- Provide students with opportunities to represent and express their prior knowledge.
- Allow students to function as designers, using tools for analyzing the world, accessing and interpreting information, organizing their personal knowledge, and representing what they know to others.
- Multimedia applications engage students and provide valuable learning opportunities.
- Empower students to create and design rather than "absorbing representations created by others".
- Encourages deep reflective thinking.
- Create personally meaningful learning.

## Educational Benefits of Multimedia from the Students Perspective

- Students that experience the technical steps needed to produce effective multimedia documents become better consumers of multimedia documents produced by others.
- Students indicate that they learn the material included in

their presentation at a much greater depth than in traditional writing projects.

- Students work with the same information from four perspectives:

(1) **As researcher**—They must locate and select the information needed to understand the chosen topic.
(2) **As authors**—They must consider their intended audience and decide what amount of information is needed to give their readers an understanding of the topic.
(3) **As designers**—They must select the appropriate media to share the concepts selected.
(4) **As writers**—They must find a way to fit the information to the container including the manner of linking the information for others to retrieve.

**Process of Applying Multimedia Approach (*See* Fig. 13.1)**

(i) At, first the terminal behaviour should be specified and defined.
(ii) The content and teaching strategies should be provided for.
(iii) Then it should be used with teaching strategies, techniques and methods.
(iv) Evaluation should be done.
(v) In the end, students should be given remedial instruction and feedback as per the diagnosis.

**Selection of Appropriate Media (*See* Figs. 13.2 & 13.3)**

A teacher must selects appropriate media approaches in order to make his/her teaching-learning process effective with the help of following points:

(1) What media approaches are available with him?
(2) In what approaches he enjoys command in application?
(3) What type of learning experiences he wants to give to the class?
(4) What teaching aids can be easily available as per that learning experience?

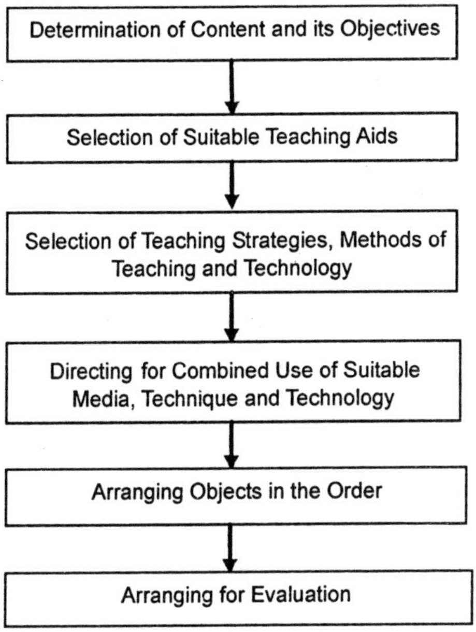


**Fig. 13.1:** Steps of Multimedia Kit Making

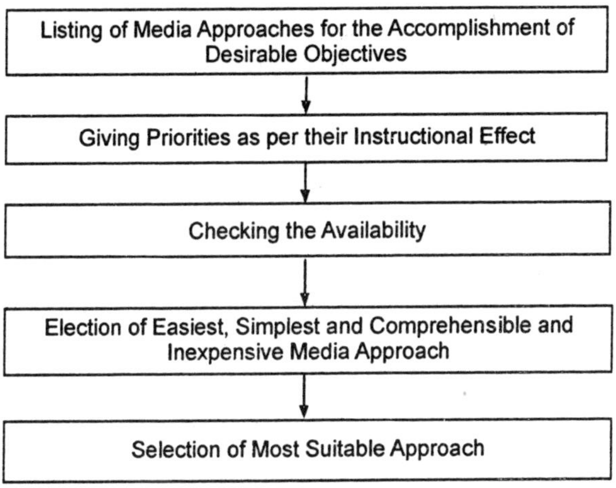


**Fig. 13.2:** Selection of Media Approaches

(5) What are the objectives of teaching a topic and what media can help to achieve them quickly?

(6) What is the class size, and what material will prove better as per it?

(7) What techniques will suit better keeping in view student's level, age, need, and rate of learning?

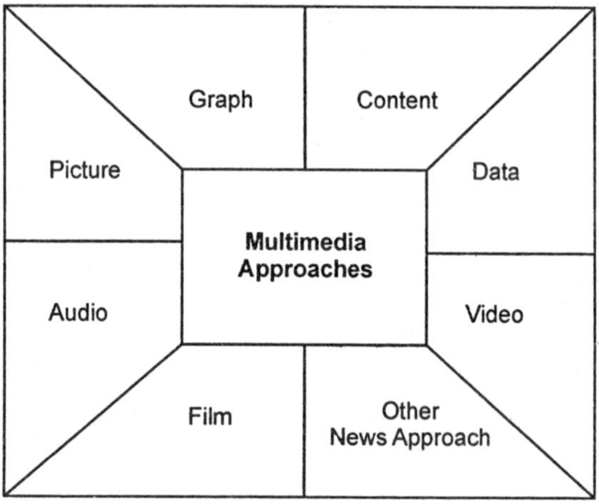


**Fig. 13.3:** Multimedia Approaches

## Benefits of Multimedia in the Classroom for Learning

The simplicity and power of multimedia enrich teacher's creativity and leads to multisensory students learning. It is also fun for qualitative improvement in teacher education in teaching-learning process. Multimedia can prove as a big breather as it is capable of sustaining the interest of the learners, through visuals and audio-inputs. It also brings in the elements of the outer world into the classroom. It can help learners in understanding the complex concepts in a very simple way. At one time, multimedia was considered to be a very technical venture. When teachers talked about using multimedia in the classroom, they probably imagined a gaggle of sophisticated components being orchestrated by a human with five or six arms. The most exciting thing about multimedia is that it reaches all the senses and that is why, its use in the field of education is even more justified.

## Conclusion

Technology is changing the classroom experience. Information and communication technology has made many innovations in teaching and learning process in order to accommodate challenging student's need. Consequently, we need to have interactive teaching and learning tools in order to ensure the learning outcomes to be achieved. Multimedia approach in teaching-learning is meant the proper and methodical application of modern technologies of communication in the field of education by which self-study can be improved and learning can be made more effective. The multimedia approach is a powerful tool in the hands of a teacher. In the multimedia approach, some techniques are used for motivation, some for giving fundamental knowledge of certain elements, some others are used for removing any misconceptions and doubts and some are used to raise the level of understanding.

## References

Benefits of using multimedia in education. www.hrsbstaff.ednet.ns.ca

*Essentials of Education Technology*—J.C. Aggarwal.

*Foundation of Educational Technology*—Dr. S.P. Kulshreshtha.

Multimedia in education-slide share. www.slideshare.net

Multimedia application for educational purposes. www.sciencedirect.com

Multimedia application for the classroom. www.cited.org

Multimedia as an Educational Tool. www.cemca.org.in

*Technological Foundation of Education*—Dr. R.A. Sharma.

Use of multimedia as a new Educational Technology. www.ijiet.org

# 14

# Technology in Classroom

## Benefits or Hindrance

*Palwinder Kaur*

### Introduction

Technology in education plays an important role in improving the educational skills and knowledge of the people. This is very important especially for those who need to improve their knowledge in order to achieve a successful life in the future. Technology in education is manifested through the use of computers. This is also a great help for teachers since, they can already enhance their teaching skills and strategies before facing their class. This technology is very essential for both the students and the teacher, but there are some instances wherein this technology is seen to be disadvantageous for both of them as well. Technology is one of the most valuable tools that we have available at our finger tips everyday. You can do virtually anything with your smart phone, tablet, or computer. Possibilities for technology are endless and not only are they endless; they are constantly improving to make the things. Many people believe that the abundance of technology in our schools is hindering students' ability to think and learn. People who support the use of technology in the classroom argue that they no longer have to rely on old style of learning.

Technology in the classroom enables the user with more interactive educational tools, which allows for a dynamic learning experience that directly benefits students. Web 2.0 interaction involves not only sharing ideas and information with someone else, but also receiving feedback. As classroom computer technology is being used for different types of communication (for presentation, for class interaction, and for collaboration), students are required to collaborate and co-create closely with others, all skills that are critical for students to learn as they grow and enter the workplace. Another advantage of using technology in the classroom is its flexibility and adaptability to differentiated learning. Technologies such as podcasts and vodcasts, for instance, provide students with the opportunity to learn at their own pace and the freedom to go back and relearn content whenever they want. This could be especially important for ESL students and students with learning disabilities: many ELL and ESL students need additional support with prononciation and defining common vocabulary that may be new to them. Other students might have difficulty in reading and reviewing complex texts. The ability to access podcasts and vodcasts on classroom computers can help address these students' needs. Using technology in the classroom, therefore, can help combat the "lecture" system of education.

## Advantages of Technology in Classroom

### *Promotes Independent learning*

Students can learn from their own even without the assistance of their parents and teachers. They are just going to surf the internet in order to look for the lessons they need to study.

### *Easier Access to Information*

The need for heavy books to be brought back and forth from school and home is no longer needed with technology. Quick accessibility is important feature of information technology which is boon for students.

### *Promotes Exciting Way to Educate Students*

Since, there are lots of images, videos, graphics and texts that are found in computer, more students feel the excitement in studying through the use of the gadget. This is very important in order to arouse their interest in studying.

### *The Information Highway*

Any question can be answered with a few clicks on the keyboard of the computer or smart phone. Powerful search engines allow an organized and simple way to find the answers that students may need for assignments or projects.

### *Broaden the Mindset*

Technology has broadened the mindsets of teachers as well as students. Before the introduction of internet students knowledge was limited up to sources around them only such as family. This caused their political and religious views to be the only ones that the family inculcates. Having access to the technology expose them to things outside of their parents interests and help them to form their own opinions.

### *Brings Some Fun in the Classroom*

Traditional learning methods make the learning monatomic and boring. This boredom turns into a lack of motivation in the students. When they are able to integrate computer learning into their normal schedule, they become much more excited to learn.

### *Helpful in Profession*

Today computer skills are required in every job earning. Teaching this skill in children will give them an extra edge which will be helpful in their profession.

### *Supports Collaboration Skills*

Students can practice collaboration skills by working in teams on projects using shared documents or conferencing technologies. This helps the students to learn to work collaboratively inside and outside classroom.

### *Increases Student Engagement and Motivation*

Technology allows teachers to engage and motivate students in new ways, like taking students on a virtual field trip to other parts of the world.

### *Provides Current Information and Wider Access*

Technology gives students the most current information available. Electronic textbooks or web-based content can provide current knowledge to searcher within no time. Classrooms can connect with other classrooms around the world to broaden learning.

### *Improves Instructional Delivery*

Teachers can design student centred lessons by allowing students to take an active part in the lesson. Classroom time can be spent with students asking critical questions and engaging in creative problem-solving.

### *Support Differentiated Instruction*

Teachers can use technology to meet the individual needs of students. Specific programmes, apps, or websites give teachers the options to offer content to students at different levels, allowing students to access material at their own pace.

### *Technology Connects with Students*

Technology occupies an important place within students' lives. By integrating technology into the classroom, teachers are changing the way they used to teach (lectures six hours a day) and providing students with the tools that will take them into the twenty-first century. Technology changes by the minute, and as educators we need to keep up with the times in order to best prepare our students for this ever-changing world in which we live.

### *Accomplishment of More Complex Tasks*

Students were able to handle more complex assignments and do more with higher-order skills because of the supports and capabilities provided by technology.

## Disadvantages of Technology in Classroom

### *Laziness in Study*

Computers make it so easy to find answers that students barely have to look upon the books for them. This may result in making the students forget the basic way of studying. Poor study habits and developing a lazy attitude towards their education.

### *Forgetting the Basic Way of Studying*

They would no longer rely on the books that are lent by their teachers for them to study, since, they are already interested to study using the computer. Even simple problems and homework that they need to answer, they are more of seeking the assistance of computers already.

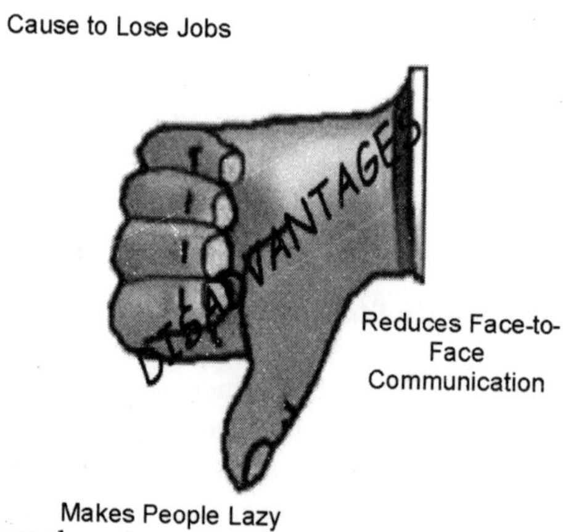


*Source:* www.google.co.in

**Fig 14.1:** Reduce Face-to-Face Communication

### *Searching for Unusual and Inappropriate Content in the Computer*

Allowing the students to surf the internet doesn't necessarily mean that all the things that they are going to discover are good for their mind and studies. The biggest concern when it comes to the use of technology in schools is how easy pornographic, violent, and other inappropriate materials can be accessed and viewed. This could cause big problems if the material is shared with other students while in the classroom; hence, they need to be properly guided by their parents and teachers.

### *Disconnected Youth*

This harmful effect of technology has already come to light in today's world. People are attached to their screens almost 24/7, which is causing an entirely new set of social issues to pop-up. This translates school system of a different way, however, more and more students are experiencing social anxieties when it comes to face-to-face interactions, but are perfectly fine socializing on-line.

### *The Cyber Bullying Trap*

Giving students access to anonymous accounts and endless contact avenues can only lead to trouble. Cyber bullying has become a real problem among youth today. This harassment has no end, which includes the classroom. There is also no way to monitor or discipline students who are involved.

### *Inevitable Cheating*

Easy access to information may seem like a great thing, it can become a real problem in a test taking environment. Cell phones have made cheating easier than ever. You no longer have to figure out how to write all of the answers down, you can just look them up!

### *A Major Distraction*

Attentiveness drops drastically in the classroom when students have their cell phones or other technologies out. The focus shifts from their teacher and education, to whatever they are looking at, playing, or doing on their phones. Despite many advantages of incorporating technology into the school curriculum and the classroom, technology can sometimes hinder learning and the educational process. Because schools occasionally purchase technology before their systems and educators are adequately equipped for and trained to use it effectively, technology sometimes goes unused or actually prevents student learning. Becoming aware of some of the disadvantages in utilizing technology in the classrooms can allow schools to better prepare for the widespread use of computers and devices by their student and teacher populations.

### *Lack of Support*

Everybody believes that technology can be a great addition to the classroom, but it can also be a source of frustration for both the teacher and the student. Unless the teacher is well trained in technology and can support the hardware in the classroom, a technology expert will be needed to troubleshoot problems. If schools cannot support the purchased technology, it essentially renders it useless in times of crisis or disrepair. Additionally, technology often needs frequent maintenance to keep it in good condition for use.

### *Inadequate Teaching Methodology*

Technology does not have a place in classrooms where teachers have not been adequately trained in its implementation. While technology is fun and can add interest for students, it is not fully integrated until students are learning from technology and not just fun with technology. In other words, using a programme to achieve a learning goal is a positive thing; however, transcending the passive use of technology and moving into active use is a skill that takes a lot of time and training.

Teaching theory behind technology education is called constructivism; teacher preparation programmes or courses in educational technology teach the concepts of inquiry-based learning. In inquiry based classrooms or lessons, students are encouraged to research topics under their own guidance and direction with teachers acting as facilitators. This type of thinking often requires great expense in terms of both money and time. Extensive professional development is required for the classroom teacher to use technology most effectively.

### *Wastage of Time*

Connection problems, downloading issues, policing software and other difficulties can cause road blocks when implementing a lesson in the technology based classroom. Teachers sometimes avoid using it simply because of lack of time. To lose 10 minutes a day or class period because of connectivity issues is not feasible, and it is one important reason why technology integration often fails in schools.

### *Maintenance Expenses*

Once technology is purchased for a school, the regular cost of maintenance is not easy to bear. Outdated software and hardware components can be incompatible with available programmes. Also, the cost of repairing broken equipment may be too expensive for school budgets. In order to be successfully implementing technology, there must be a rolling replacement or updating plan in place to keep technology current and useful.

### *Incompatibility Issues*

Many schools today have curricula and programmes-based on state or national assessments. The majority of these tests and measures are paper-and-pencil-based in order-to-make them accessible for all students and schools.

## Conclusion

Impact of technology in schools is somewhere between it is the only way to make a positive change in schools to it is a new fad. Technology is a strong tool for positive change, but it must be presented in the right ways. When students are using technology as a tool or a support for communicating with others, they are in an active role rather than the passive role of recipient of information transmitted by a teacher, textbook, or broadcast. The student is actively making choices about how to generate, obtain, manipulate, or display information. Technology allows many more students to be actively thinking about information, making choices, and executing skills than is typical in teacher-led lessons. Moreover, when technology is used as a tool to support students in performing authentic tasks, the students are in the position of defining their goals, making decisions, and evaluating their progress. The teacher's role changes as well. The teacher is no longer the centre of attention as the dispenser of information, but rather plays the role of facilitator, setting project goals and providing guidelines and resources, moving from student to student or group to group, providing suggestions and support for student activity. As students work on their technology-supported products, the teacher rotates through the room, looking over shoulders, asking about the reasons for various design choices, and suggesting resources that might be used. Project based work and cooperative learning approaches prompt this change in roles, whether technology is used or not. However, tool uses of technology are highly compatible with this new teacher role, since they stimulate so much active mental work on the part of students. Moreover, when the venue for work is technology, the teacher often finds him or herself joined by many peer coaches' students who are technology savvy and eagre to share their knowledge with others.

## References

Greenhow, C., Robelia, B., and Hughes, J.E. (2009). Web 2.0 and classroom research: What path should we take now? *Educational Researcher*, 38(4): 246-259.

Hmaisat, H. (1990). Introduction of computers in secondary schools in Jordan. *International Journal of Instructional Media*, 17(1): 73-82.

Mckenzie, J. (1999), *How Teachers Learn Technology Best*, Twiggs Company.

Wang, L., Ertmer, A.P., and Newby, J.T. (2004). Increasing Preservice Teachers' Self-Efficacy Beliefs for Technology Integration. *Journal of Research on Technology in Education*, 36(3).

# Index